The Highly Opinionated Newsletter

The Highly Opinionated Newsletter

A Sometimes Judicious Sometimes Injudicious DISSENT From the Majority Opinion on the Current Art Scene

Volumes One and Two

Gentle Indignation

Writers Club Press
San Jose New York Lincoln Shanghai

The Highly Opinionated Newsletter
A Sometimes Judicious
Sometimes Injudicious
DISSENT
From the Majority Opinion on the Current Art Scene

Writers Club Press
an imprint of iUniverse, Inc.

For information address:
iUniverse, Inc.
5220 S. 16th St., Suite 200
Lincoln, NE 68512
www.iuniverse.com

ISBN: 0-595-21899-7

Printed in the United States of America

CONTENTS

TABLE OF ILLUSTRATIONS

ACKNOWLEDGEMENTS

I wish to acknowledge the help of my husband, Chuck, for his efforts and encouragement in putting this book together. With some help from our daughter, Jill, he spent hours preparing the material for press. He designed and wrote the text on the back cover. And, finally, it was his decision to select and include the beautiful illustrations, a process which required exhaustive research.

INTRODUCTION

These reviews are written as a way of both collecting my thoughts and recording them. The reviews follow these two guidelines, First, to keep each review simple and readable. And, second, to limit each review to one or two pages in length. As a reviewer, I have noticed an abundance of scholarly reviews and historical analyses, some valuable, some merely obtuse. As an artist, neither my background, expertise nor inclination leads me in this direction.

So my intentions differ. My first intention is to provide an overview of a practicing artist. This overview is naturally subjective and personal. It reflects my belief that art is of vital importance in our lives. That art exists to nourish us and to connect us to a dimension larger than the one in which many of us may conduct our daily lives.

My second intention, which I feel is just as important, is to question what goes on in the current art scene. Historically, what is promoted on the art scene results from a consensus of the art establishment. This is as true today as it always has been. What is different are the standards, or lack of historical standards, that now apply.

The aesthetic today forms a radical break with aesthetics of the past. The present vogue is for innovation and sensation. But what may be innovative or sensational at one time becomes familiar and unsensational in another. How is it possible to separate what will be remembered from what is forgettable and will be forgotten? Or is it possible? Gertrude Stein claimed that "a museum of modern art is an oxymoron." Perhaps she was right. Perhaps only the judgment of subsequent centuries will tell.

These are the issues which I feel are not being addressed today. These are the issues which I try to address in my newsletter. My attempts are the result of decades of painting and decades of looking at art. They are the result of caring and thinking deeply. They involve the combined judgments of my eye and my mind and my heart.

The opinions expressed range from the reverent to the irreverent. Some of you will agree with what I write. Many of you will disagree. My hope is that, whatever your own final opinion may be, each one of you will discover something of value through the process.

Gentle Indignation   April 2002

The term Gentle Indignation pays homage, and alludes, to "Savage Indignation", the designation appropriated by the great English satirist Jonathan Swift.

The author reserves the right to omit any review when it is appropriate to do so.

I wish to thank my personal assistant, without whose devoted efforts these essays could not have been published. Moreover, I seek to persuade him to contribute his trenchant comments to future editions, under the pen name he himself has selected: Querulous Dissent.

And, finally, I would like to add special thanks to my daughter, Jill, whose always astonishing computer skills are invaluable to the success of so many of my enterprises.

Volume One

Rembrandt at the
Metropolitan Museum of Art

December, 1995

The Highly Opinionated Newsletter

Volume One, Number 1

Rembrandt-not Rembrandt at MMA—This exhibition, based upon a reevaluation of Rembrandt's work, presents the viewer with one difficulty after another. Various scholars engage in a dialogue intended to demonstrate that reattribution of Rembrandt's work is a science. They demonstrate instead that it is an art. If not an educated guessing game. We become aware both how inconclusive are the results of the technology that these scholars employ and how insufficient it is to resolve dispute. And so all efforts to show how **objective** this process is demonstrate unequivocally, if unintentionally, how **subjective** it is. Even at times—dare we say it—arbitrary.

Each scholar expounds his **own** reasons by which to justify his **own** preferences and his **own** conclusions. But their reasons vary and their conclusions differ. Moreover, in many cases, conclusions accepted for centuries are overturned. And we can't help wondering whether they won't be overturned yet again. It is utter confusion.

Throughout the career of most artists, style and direction will vary, as will degree of success. In this century one may note the work of Picasso and Mondrian among others. Analysis of some work is not always relevant to analysis of other work. Any procedure which fails to take this into account can do disservice, not only to the scholarship process, but also to the artist himself.

In this exhibit, Rembrandt's hand is disputed everywhere. We start to question how accurate these assessments are and even to question whether some genuine work may be inadvertently discarded. It is all quite disheartening. I disagreed with so many decisions that I started to wonder whether a procedure so unable to decide exactly what any artist did or did not do may not somehow tarnish both his originality **and** his genius.

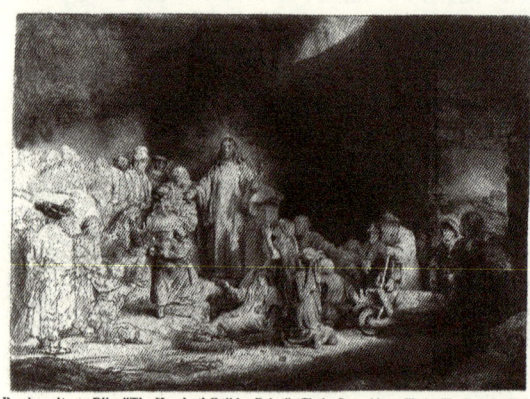

Rembrandt van Rijn, "The Hundred Guilder Print" (Christ Preaching; Christ Healing the Sick), ca. 1643–49 [etching with drypoint & burin, 2nd state of 2; 11" x 15"]

Greatly to my relief, I found the great *Hundred Guilder Print* untouched. As of now, the scholars are leaving it alone. As of now it is still safely ensconced among the diminishing body of Rembrandt's recognized work. For the time being it is still conceded to be the real thing by the masterly —if no longer inimitable —hand of this artist.

Gentle Indignation   December 1995

Mondrian at the Museum of Modern Art

December, 1995

The Highly Opinionated Newsletter

Volume One, Number 2

Mondrian at MOMA—This exhibit traces Mondrian's strange artistic journey from representation to abstraction, from fullness to emptiness.

Early Mondrian is as skilled as is the later work, in both composition and color. But the early canvases are saturated with representation and emotion. Signs of his later concerns with abstraction and order are present, of course, but they are not present to the exclusion of all else. Landscapes are romantic, at times overly so. Many share an emphasis on effects of light and silhouette, with lush darks contrasted against richly hued sky; others emphasize pattern and symmetry. A group of canvases from 1908–9 finds the artist experimenting with the use of dots and dashes. Color here frequently becomes too decorative and too pretty, and work from these years becomes more successful as shape and color simplify.

Mondrian's mature style develops over the course of the following decade. In 1911, geometric lines begin to allude to subject matter in an interesting, but still recognizable way. By 1914, any reference to nature, which contains no lines, is made—paradoxically—through a series of vertical and horizontal grids. By 1917, explicitly recognizable subject matter is banished altogether and nature, specifically, is eliminated from the work. Conceptualization replaces representation, and, for the first time in Mondrian, design itself becomes content.

The style upon which Mondrian's reputation rests has now been formed. This style consists of the following characteristics. Exploration of formal relationships replaces exploration of nature. Visual content, and with it tension, disappears. Surface becomes everything and although it is handsome—at times even elegant—surface concentration simply lacks depth. Calculation replaces spontaneity, and so animation yields to the inanimate. A certain purity *does* result, but so does a sterility. Art has become so intellectualized as to be rendered devoid of all currents of emotional resonance or richness.

The effects of such an attempt to redefine art seem utterly barren, for what has been produced is the result of measurement. In science, to measure is to know. But this is not true for art. Art is about feeling, and Mondrian has substituted measurement for feeling. Art has been deconstructed. It has been depleted of the singular essence that makes it art.

In the 1942 *Boogie Woogie*, Mondrian breaks line into primary color and a new rhythmic sense and playfulness appear. But does this constitute art? Do playfulness and rhythm constitute content? Can they compensate for lack of content? And, even more importantly, without content, can vision exist? Comparison of the cartoon of any Mondrian grid with any Renaissance cartoon more than suffices to show what has been lost. And what has been lost seems immeasurably greater than whatever has been gained in this dubious process of aesthetic cleansing.

Surely there is a point at which less is no longer more, but at which less is simply less. And surely, if this point exists, for me Mondrian has passed it.

Gentle Indignation   **December 1995**

VERMEER AT THE NATIONAL GALLERY OF ART

December, 1995

The Highly Opinionated Newsletter

Volume One, Number 3

Vermeer at the National Gallery of Art—This exhibit brings together 21 of 35 known Vermeers, and confirms the artist's devotion to the poetry of the everyday. Vermeer is a magician whose brush transforms all that it touches. Through the medium of flowing light, Vermeer modifies color and orchestrates composition. There is a hush to the paintings—the stillness of a momentary glance or action arrested forever. The figures are placed in interior spaces, the geometry of which functions like a setting for jewels. These settings, often with lush fabrics delineating recessed areas, are about privacy. However a window or a map always connects these figures to an external world. The interior setting is highly ordered. Geometry patterns the floor and walls and the very panes of the windows admitting light. Emotional life is merely hinted at. Instead, Vermeer's figures concentrate intensely on whatever they are doing, both subsumed by and connected to some context larger than themselves.

Early and late Vermeers seem relatively flawed. But the work of the 1650's and 60's is wondrous. The single disappointment for me, among work from these years, was *View of Delft*. I found Vermeer's usually unerring sense of color unification to be missing. Dense, opaque reflections in the foreground did not capture the extraordinary Vermeer luminosity of the scintillating overcast sky. So unaccustomed was my eye to the imbalance I perceived, that I could scarcely stop wondering whether this work had not undergone color restoration.

Little Street is a beautiful, geometric dance of shape, a wondrous interplay of form. Arches and rectangles are ordered, reordered, then fragmented into series of still smaller units. A single red shutter ignites the composition. Patterned doorways—usually points of entry—serve to compartmentalize, separate, and finally link the various small figures busily engaged in work. The entire scene has an air of both liveliness and of peace.

Just as extraordinary is *Young Woman with Water Pitcher*. The woman is solid. Yet she is simultaneously monumentalized and dematerialized by the light around her. As she pauses momentarily, her fingers resting on the windowpane, she becomes both connected to and a conduit for the light. Here, in the simplest of ways, Vermeer somehow links the corporeal and the incorporeal. The woman and the light source are one.

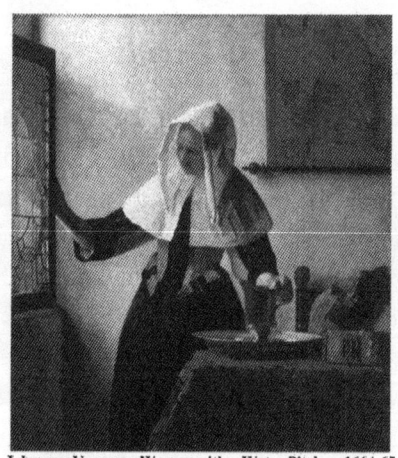

Johannes Vermeer, Woman with a Water Pitcher, 1664-65 [oil on canvas; 46" x 42"]

Girl With the Pearl Earring is painted with scarcely a line or an edge, the head a composite of light-filled planes that emerge and dissolve. Only the shadow of a lid, nostril, ear and neck provide delicate, if distinct, contour. And that is sufficient. The eyes gaze at us through the centuries, and as we are gathered into their gaze, we are deeply touched.

This exhibit has allowed us to enter Vermeer's world, a world fabricated

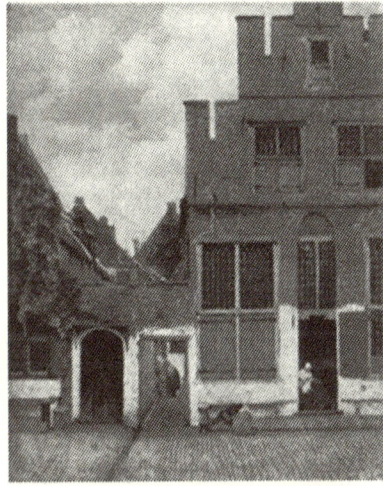

Johannes Vermeer, The Little Street, 1657-58
[oil on canvas; 54" x 44 "]

of geometry and of light. These two very different elements are each essential to a vision combining the worldly and the otherworldly, the timely and the timeless. For it is Vermeer's unique achievement to see in the ordinary that which is extraordinary; to see in the secular that which is divine; to use light itself as a means of transfiguration; and to find in a moment all of eternity.

Gentle Indignation   **December 1995**

JOSEPH CORNELL AT THE WHITNEY MUSEUM

January, 1996

The Highly Opinionated Newsletter

Volume One, Number 4

Joseph Cornell at the Whitney—This small selection of Cornell work acts as a fine introduction to the artist's rarefied world, a world in which celestial and terrestrial realms are contemplated, contrasted and inter-connected. It is a world of space—to which maps of the heavens, the zodiac, and the constellations are guides. And it is a world of time—the presence of the past is everywhere. But it is also a world transcending space and time —a world of being—to which geometric symbols, iconic items, and various indecipherable elements serve as clues.

The artist uses paper reproductions taken from antiquity, nature, and the world of ballet, and he also uses ordinary found objects. They are fashioned into meticulous collages or into the boxlike constructions for which he is best known. The work usually contains disparate elements, arranged in ways that never quite coexist. The impact varies. Some of the pieces are either too obvious or too obscure. But most are tantalizing.

For Cornell's small worlds entice even as they elude the intellect: they are worlds that can never be fully seen. Grids, peepholes, and shifting sand contain or conceal them. Mirrors reveal to us how much of what We perceive is a product of self–reflection.

The artist's language is symbolic and metaphysical. Geometric forms such as spheres and spirals appear repeatedly, often changing in scale. Natural shapes are juxtaposed with man–made objects. Ordinary pipes are painted white and broken, rendered as fragile as memories eroded by time. Wine glasses are placed in rows, revealing odd contents—bits and pieces of nature. Open expanses are contained; vastness is measured and chained. Sky cedes to sand, sand cedes to sky, as everything connects and intermingles.

Hotel du Nord, with its mythic constellation, acts as an enclosure for universal emptiness. *Celestial Navigation* links varied forms of heaven and earth. In *Untitled*, the human mind is set among the very abstractions it creates and ponders, itself yet another container, an exemplar of that which is abstract.

Joseph Cornell at C & M Arts—Cornell's explorations continue here. Not all the work is of high quality and the collages in particular seem of lesser interest.

In the most successful boxes, dualities are examined and transformed— light is contrasted with dark, science with art. A white pipe lies under the skies, broken—a symbol of the fragility of man's efforts to fathom space and conquer time. Wine glasses line up in neatly ordered rows, but their contents obey no rules of logic. Mind continues to measure and to categorize in its extraordinary effort to comprehend the incomprehensible and to grasp the ungraspable.

For despite all attempts of science and art to understand, in the end there remains only the mystery. And it is this mystery—of the finite and the infinite each infusing the other—into which the art and the boxes of Joseph Cornell delve.

Gentle Indignation   **January 1996**

BRANCUSI AT THE MUSEUM OF MODERN ART

March, 1996

The Highly Opinionated Newsletter

Volume One, Number 5

Brancusi at MOMA—This selection of 24 sculptures forms a dramatic introduction to the artist's work. Arrayed as they are on strange and unusual pedestals, Brancusi's sculpturally streamlined forms take on a new appearance. No longer does the simplified shape of the object dominate. Instead, the work fuses into something else entirely. Combining a pared–down concept with an elaborate presentation, it forms a larger sculptural presence. Sculpture and pedestal can no longer be considered separate entities: they must be viewed as one.

This seems to be the predominant feature of an exhibit which requires some reassessment of the artist's work. Do these elegant shapes fit with their contrasting pedestals? How? Why does the artist choose to present them this way? What is being accomplished?

The work as a whole seems to acquire an eerie, otherworldly presence. Sculpture contrasts with pedestal in terms of shape and material. Pedestal shapes vary from whimsically free form to strictly geometric. Coolness of sculptured metal sparkles against dulled warmth of wood.

The shaped oval is fundamental to this artist and it is a theme he uses over and over again. *Mademoiselle Pogany*, a metal oval, has a lovely grace; while the wood *Chief*—an oval with a tiny crown and large moon–sliced mouth—is altogether comic. *Two Muses* differ only in the materials from which they are made: yet the shiny oval muse seems bold; the plaster one shy. The oval head of a *Child*, carved of darkly textured wood, seems mysterious. *Blond Negress* is a medley of ovals repeated to form head, hair and lips. Its anthropomorphic pedestal suggests a torso. My favorite of the oval sculptures was *Young Bird*, an oval with an oval slice. Upon its cubed and cylindrical pedestal, it looks just as if it were perched in its own nest on its own tree.

Many pieces work well visually. Others did not work for me. I found both *Timidity* and *Exotic Plant* to be ungainly in shape and proportion, and not understandable without titles.

Possibly the two most beautiful works are *Fish* and *Bird in Space*. *Fish* is a flat oblong poised horizontally over three circular bases. The gray–white markings of its marble suggest water. Its shape resembles the prow of a boat cleaving waves. The overall impression is one of hovering motion. *Bird in Space* is a vertical sweep in gold. Curved and pointed, it strains upward against the cubed pedestals which anchor it.

And so Brancusi creates a world in which object is inextricably linked to presentation. The question occurs, how much is art? how much is presentation? Is it possible that neither sculpture nor pedestal functions fully without the other; that only together does each become whole? When such a concept works, the piece can be extraordinary. But there are times

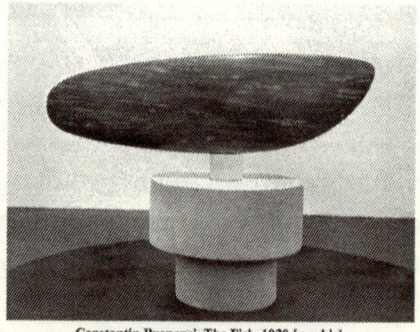

Constantin Brancusi, The Fish, 1930 [marble]

when I wondered whether the concept *did* work; whether, instead, each part was simply incomplete. Were simplification and repetition of form overdone? Was too much being asked of too little? I have not fully resolved such questions. But it does seem to me that although Brancusi's world can exert a spell which is wondrous, it can also display a tedious sameness which is not.

Gentle Indignation March 1996

THE CHATSWORTH COLLECTION AT THE MORGAN LIBRARY

April, 1996

The Highly Opinionated Newsletter

Volume One, Number 6

The Chatsworth Collection at the Morgan Library—As is true of virtually all Renaissance drawings, these are of extraordinary quality. Draftsmanship of even minor artists is on a level rarely seen today. Skills in every area—anatomy, modeling, perspective, and composition—abound. And yet, as this exhibit demonstrates once again, such skills diminish in meaning when not directed toward some other purpose. For skill employed as an end, rather than as a means toward something larger than skill, results in an art that is always academic.

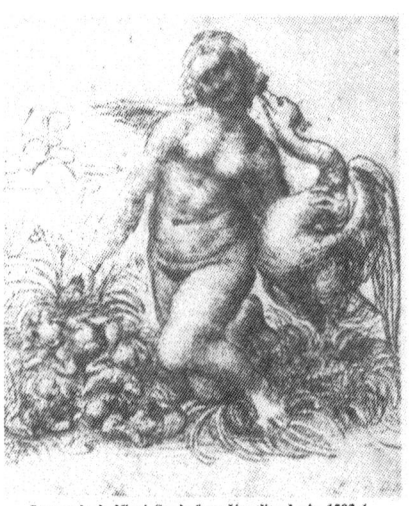

Leonardo da Vinci, Study for a Kneeling Leda, 1503-4
[pen over wash; 6¼" x 5½"]

The Renaissance, a celebration above all of the human figure, reached an artistic zenith in Italy. Much strength was apparent in the wonderful Italian drawings on view, as in a Parmigianino *Bearded Figure Sleeping*, power rippling through the well-muscled figure in repose. But other work suffered from too much technique or else faltered conceptually. In a set of Fra Lippo Lippi studies, the folds of the garments were developed with such attention as nearly to overwhelm the graceful figures. A

Ghirlandaio *Head of a Woman* seemed somewhat prosaic without the luminous color of his paintings. In a rare Leonardo study of *Leda and the Swan**, the swan displayed almost phallic qualities and the duo itself formed an undulating erotic whole. But the work, while a fascinating treatment of mythology, presented strange problems: Leda's torso was flaccid, and her right hand alarmingly inverted. At their worst, Italian drawings are needlessly complex and ornate. An example of this was Veronese's *Allegory to Celebrate the Publication of the Holy League*, in which even the title shares these faults; another was a Passeri drawing, in which figures posture and simper sentimentally.

The few examples of French landscapes seemed to suffer from a generally florid quality.

The selection on the Northern Renaissance displayed again both strengths and weaknesses. The Goltzius was a work of visual excess. Durer's *Women's Public Bath*, with its remarkable precision, became a clever occasion to caricature youth and old age. Van Dyck was represented by several works. Both *Head and Forequarters of a Horse* and *Landscape* were delicately abstracted, and a pair of portraits was insightful as well as beautifully drawn.

But among all the work, the Raphaels and the Rembrandts seemed most to reach a completion.

---

* The author was referred by the Morgan Library to a noted art historian, Leo Steinberg, with questions about this drawing. After analyzing such elements as poor draftsmanship, anatomical slackness, inconsistencies of cross-hatching and shading, a conclusion was reached that its authenticity was dubious.

The Raphaels were transcendent for their grace of line and distillation. Each of the four drawings was tautly focused. In *Study for a Battle Scene*, everything—torsos, limbs, shadows—contributed a rhythmic quality to an abstractly diagonal composition, in which foreground fades softly through barely delineated figures. In *Study of a Transfigured Head*, sensitively modeled planes impart an ethereal quality to a youth glancing over his shoulder with downcast eyes.

Even more extraordinary were the Rembrandts—four landscapes and a portrait. Like the works of Raphael, they, too, are touching in their simplicity. But they have, in addition, a sense of intimacy and introspection unique to this artist. Their smallness somehow encompass the sadness of the world. Their large expanse of empty space evokes a transience and fragility. Line appears spontaneous, richly varied in width and shading. Here, a Rembrandt landscape acts as a microcosm for all of nature and the human condition. And, in a portrait of an *Actor*, Rembrandt evokes an interior life of lonely self-awareness, conveying it through gesture and expression with such economy that it is breathtaking.

Gentle Indignation   **April 1996**

SPLENDORS OF IMPERIAL CHINA AT THE METROPOLITAN MUSEUM

May, 1996

The Highly Opinionated Newsletter

Volume One, Number 7

Splendors of Imperial China: Treasures from the National Palace Museum, Taipei—This was perhaps too extensive an exhibit, covering too extensive a subject—the arts of China—and the array of items on view was huge, consisting of icons, ornaments, pottery, vessels, painting and calligraphic scrolls. Since the exhibit was more comprehensive than selective, it was impossible on a single visit to view more than a fraction of the pieces. Of those I saw, most were of extremely beautiful workmanship, with a spiritual dimension elevating both object and viewer.

One of the first objects on view in the galleries—and certainly one of the loveliest—was the *Pi*, a jade disc. With utter simplicity of shape and material, it reached a standard that few objects here or elsewhere ever do. A central space was surrounded by a pale circle of jade, the textural and contour irregularities of which bear a touching reminder of the passage of time. With its contrasting solid and space, the piece seemed almost an allusion to yin and yang, as well as to immortality and decline.

Pottery, calligraphy and drawing are all major art forms. Pottery ranges from the simple geometry of the 12th century Sung period to complex designs in which shape, pattern and color are intricately linked. Geometric pottery attains a purity, while more complicated pottery has an excitement, and each offers a distinctive reward. With elegant symbols, calligraphy creates an entire world, its fascination heightened by the impenetrability of that world to western eyes. At their best, line drawings possess a startling purity, and a bamboo stand depicted in shades of gray may elicit a profound meditation on all of nature. Portraits of rulers—intended to personalize, commemorate and monumentalize—while quite imposing, can often appear stilted, one-dimensional and illustrational.

However, the aesthetic culmination for me resides, without doubt, in this culture's extraordinary landscape painting. Chinese landscape is never really about place; it is about philosophy. It is about the infinitude of nature and the transience of man; about nature's eternal cycles and the limited seasons of our own small lives. Sung landscapes in particular are among the most extraordinary created anywhere anytime. A 12th century anonymous *Landscape* had a quiet splendor—filled with finely delineated rocks, trees, mountains and small houses, each composed of finely differentiated strokes. Its vertical shape gave it a gentle upward sweep, as of an ascending spiritual path. In a later 14th century landscape scroll by Huang Kung-wang, mountains alternated with empty tracts, and a horizontal path along the water's edge seemed to refer again to the poignancy of our own human journey—a journey ending always in a vast and ultimate void.

But from the 15th century onward, a noticeable coarsening appears. Line becomes less refined, pattern becomes too busy, and the introduction of color only increases decorative aspects and prettiness. By the 17th century, Ching Dynasty, the influence from the West is even greater, bringing with it even more elaborate and gaudy elements. And so here, before our eyes, we view with dismay the gradual erosion of a once remarkable and singular vision.

Gentle Indignation   **April 1996**

HOMER AT THE METROPOLITAN MUSEUM

June, 1996

The Highly Opinionated Newsletter

Volume One, Number 8

Winslow Homer at MMA—The most surprising thing about this exhibit was the almost total lack of surprise. Instead of growth and development, there was throughout a strange sense of stasis almost from the first work to the last.

Homer's origin was as an illustrator, and this training served too well, for he never veered far—or far enough—from it. He learned to paint everything with remarkable verisimilitude, and almost always did. Composition, draftsmanship, light and shade are admirable, but the irony of the extraordinary technique he relies upon is this: the more he relies upon it, the more it limits him. He seldom uses it as a means of exploring or stretching boundaries, and so technique itself *becomes* the boundary.

The content of Homer's work forms a narrative of America, but it is a narrative steeped in sentiment and nostalgia, in heroism and mythology. The mythology is about American virtue and American valor, and to the extent that these traits are idealized, they are falsified and rendered trite.

For Homer's major appeal is also his major flaw: the world he paints and the people in it are always picturesque. In his imaginary America, every child is innocent, every man heroic, and every woman beautiful. He chronicles events so curiously that a Civil War soldier sniping in a tree looks as unconcerned and picturesque as if he were engaged in some pastoral activity. Women at work are always picturesque, too, posing in a picturesque world filled with picturesque details—down to the picturesque laces and soles of their picturesque shoes. Men are engaged either in manly pursuits, in rescuing women, or in fearlessly confronting picturesque elements. And it is not be missed how—even *in extremis*—everyone is picturesquely posed in either a sensuous or virile way.

Here and there, a painting overcomes these flaws. The 1869–70 beach scenes have an air of spontaneity as playful groups of figures splash color splotches against the blue of sea and sky. The 1878 *Waiting for Boats* acquires fluidity through an omission of detail. *Houses on a Hill* (1879) is set in an atmosphere of shimmering sunlight; while *Eastern Point Light* (1880) projects a subtle poetry. An 1881 sketch of *Fishermen*, with clustered figures, strikes a somber note, and an 1880 watercolor, *St. John's River, Florida*, with verticals of reflected trees, has a delicate calligraphic quality.

My two favorites were early work. In *Artist Sketching in White Mountains* (1868), a pair of white umbrellas trace a sun-filled diagonal against an arching sky. And the 1867 *Studio* is a rich medley of russets against which two backlit musicians play their music in rapt attention.

Gentle Indignation   **June 1996**

Cézanne at the Philadelphia Museum of Art

July, 1996

The Highly Opinionated Newsletter

Volume One, Number 9

Cézanne at the Philadelphia Museum of Art—Cézanne's world is a remarkable one, wrought like architecture from blocks of color and planes, then synthesized into a vision encompassing all of nature. From a tentative beginning, then with unexpected swiftness, a vision startlingly new and entirely his own appeared. Color lightened and brightened; brush transformed subject matter into rhythmic and interlocking planes; and the whole became immersed in a radiant, cool blue light.

Yet, the Philadelphia exhibit, while assembling work from all stages of the artist's life, failed to develop the extraordinary sense of excitement and artistic culmination that other exhibits have conveyed. Opening galleries presented too much early work, which was somber, turgid, rawly emotional, and didn't quite work on any level. The cumulative effect was rather depressing, the chief curiosity being that it was painted by Cézanne at all. Far too crowded together in the last gallery were far too few of the beautiful late works. Even with familiar and representative canvases on view, a full sense of genius never unfolded. Whether this was due to the installation, the pattern of traffic flow, or the absence of particular works, I am not sure.

Cézanne portraits—either of himself or of others—are quite enigmatic. The subject's personality is almost always inaccessible, of less concern than the exploration of surface as a series of planes. The portrait is a means of evasion rather than of revelation. There is a kind of modern alienation: a sense of disorientation as subject is turned into object—an unknown and unknowable other.

Throughout the years, the figure as bather obsessed the artist. Here, too, it is difficult to fathom just what such figures mean. Are they modern counterparts to the tradition of nudes in an idyllic setting? Are they studies of the figure as part of, yet distinct from, nature? Are they an occasion to shift and abstract the female form? An occasion to desentimentalize the feminine? Some or none of the above? It is hard to tell. Although these are regarded as major works, I found them difficult to like, which may, after all, be their point.

Cézanne's still lifes, worlds in themselves, are unlike any other still lifes ever painted. For one thing, they are seldom still. They are dynamic entities, surging with energy and pulsing with color. Composition follows a general format. Most canvases contain a horizontal surface; a background—often patterned; a tablecloth with folds less observed than asserted; and varied objects and clusters of fruit. Yet this simple format permits a powerful exploration into form. Fruit is broken into sophisticated planes of color, both delicate and intense, and becomes a sensual focal point as well as an anchor in an ordered but vibrant world.

A Cézanne landscape, like great art anywhere, defies definition or explanation. The artist analyzes at the same time as he constructs a vision of nature, using color and plane. Shape is built upon shape until form emerges. The paintings of the Mont Sainte-Victoire series, especially, become astonishing transfigurations in which land, sky and mountain alternately merge or contrast. In a dazzling display of art as alchemy, the artist experiments with endless contrasts of horizontal or vertical, dark or light, muted or glowing, solid or transparent.

As is true for many great artists, the late years brought with them an astonishing breakthrough. Through the medium of watercolor, the artist distilled his vision to the essential: a vision of transcendent emptiness. Line is now completed through suggestion; color is now defined by absence; reduction and synthesis now occur simultaneously. The vision is of a reality underlying, beyond and greater than visible reality, a vision of the not-there in the there. Parts coalesce into something greater than themselves, indicating a reality that can be understood—if at all—only through a manifestation of those parts.

Gentle Indignation   **July 1996**

Picasso at the Museum of Modern Art

July, 1996

The Highly Opinionated Newsletter

Volume One, Number 10

Picasso and Portraiture at the Museum of Modern Art—The tragedy of Picasso was this. By the age of twenty, he could do all there was to do and knew all there was to know in art. But thereafter, he would spend the rest of his life trying to find something worthwhile to say. His gifts were prodigious—gifts given to few —but he never possessed a singular vision commensurate with those gifts. Rather, he would go off in too many different directions saying too many different things. At times his personal life became so entwined with his art that his art became a mirror of that life merely. The reflection was not pretty. For his personal life was a morass. And as he fled from woman to woman in a vain attempt to satisfy some insatiable need, both he and the art in which he chronicled this flight turned bitter and mocking.

This exhibit consists mostly of portraits of these women. The works, bursting with power and energy, record gigantic, often conflicting desires. They show a hunger never satisfied over a quest never resolved. The resulting tension is a source of immense creativity and fascination, while the continuous lack of resolution is a major flaw.

The selection of portraits reveals high points as well as lows. Picasso's journey begins with a measure of self-acceptance and peace. Before long, an uneasiness manifests—a sense of loneliness, isolation and longing. This receives tender and poignant expression in works from the blue period and in those of the circus world. Thereafter, a growing frustration appears, and as relationship after relationship sours, the artist turns upon both himself and the women whom he fails and is failed by. The paintings reflect this, becoming ever more distorted and contrived. Surprisingly, a repetition of vocabulary and theme sets in, and the art, while retaining its vigor, starts to seem formulaic and stale.

Throughout the artist's career, drawings invariably possess vitality, beauty or humor—and at times also incorporate a personal philosophy. In this exhibit, the 1928–30 *Marie Therese in a Beret*, an exquisite portrait of his mistress, displays the classical mastery that Picasso could summon at will. Other drawings of Marie Therese have a similar deftness, as in the charming bewilderment expressed in *Marie Therese Considering her Sculpted Effigy*. The double portrait of *Diaghilev and Seligsburg* (1921) also has a wonderful sense of élan. And a still earlier work, *Appolinaire* (1905–8), reveals a delicious sense of caricature and wit.

Early paintings are fresh and exploratory. The 1905 *Woman in a Chemise*—a profile in whites and blues—is simple, placid and mysterious. *Seated Nude*—in reds, grays and flesh tones applied seemingly at random —possesses grace in face and gesture.

Pablo Picasso, Portrait of Gertrude Stein, 1906 [oil on canvas; 39¼" x 32"]

The 1906 *Gertrude Stein* created a stir during the artist's lifetime. This portrait abstracts and simplifies and produces a masklike effect. But I found the effect to be enigmatic and the character to be impenetrable. The 1910 synthetic cubist *Girl With a Mandolin* is a rhythmic interplay in subtle ochres and grays, with a lilt that somehow evokes both music and musician.

Canvases from the 1920's can be quite tender, as in the 1923 *Paulo on a Donkey* and two *Mother and Child* paintings of 1922: one a study in warm reds and ochres, the other in cool greens and blues. The first seems to refer to the world of emotions, the second to a more placid world of nature. Sara Murphy is the 1923 *Woman in White*, a work of serene beauty brushed in with elegant line upon a brownish-green and white ground. The eyes and long waving hair are quite gentle. And a 1923 *Harlequin* gazes past the canvas edge. He is a figure ironically lost in a private reverie while costumed for a role on-stage.

The 1930's mark a change. Occasionally there is still work of great delicacy, as in the *Nusch Eluard* paintings. But the delicacy seems linked to distance in relationship. Otherwise a new bitterness appears. Portraits of Picasso's child Maya have a decidedly nasty edge. And portraits of Dora Maar turn grotesque in proportion as his affection for her wanes. The terrible transformations which she undergoes in paint imply a deep underlying cruelty in the artist.

Works from the 1940's and 50's depicting the artist's relationships with Françoise Gilot and Jacqueline are frequently valid and occasionally lovely. A 1954 portrait of Jacqueline, with elongated neck and oval eye, is particularly arresting in the bold simplicity of its color and shape.

But soon there is startling evidence of decline and strain, and everything, even invention, seems to fail the artist. As he struggles on, the 60's yield a group of work that can be considered only embarrassing.

Perhaps three self-portraits most succinctly sum up Picasso's progression. An early 1901 *Self-Portrait* with blue-white face and pink lips has a haunted look. In a 1918 pencil study, large prominent eyes are earnest and searching. But by 1972, the face is quite transformed. It has now become a sweep of thickened lines encircling a pair of startled eyes that gaze out at us in total and abject despair.

Gentle Indignation   **July 1996**

Rembrandt at the Dyansen Gallery

August, 1996

The Highly Opinionated Newsletter

Volume One, Number 11

Rembrandt Etchings at the Dyansen Gallery—Etching is a medium in which Rembrandt excels. This small selection shows the artist in varying moods. His subject matter embraces the entire human condition. Here are the poor and the well-to-do, the humble and the assured, the worldly and the spiritual. All are viewed as participants in a shared humanity.

Throughout his etchings, Rembrandt demonstrates a mastery of line and composition, of light and shade, and of expression and gesture. Just as masterly is his use of space. Empty space forms an integral part of the work, functioning so as to expand and order the composition in much the same way as light does. Space serves not only as a means of contrast, but also as a visual respite to pattern and detail. Groups are composed of individualized figures. Such groups often contrast with and further isolate the central figure.

Secular etchings are lively. In *Beggar Woman*, the shaded silhouette of a woman merges playfully with the folds of her garment.

Religious pieces function in ways that transcend literal subject matter. Incidents are raised to a higher symbolic and spiritual framework, so that every scene, figure or action acquires universal significance. The tender *Circumcision* alludes to both the mystery and origin of all that is divine. *Christ Driving the Money Changers from the Temple* becomes a ritual of purification and of reclaiming spiritual space. *The Raising of Lazarus*—with its large area devoted to a symbolically looming rock—is about faith in divinity and in the miracle of immortality. The *Beheading of John the Baptist* speaks of poise and equanimity when faced with death. *Agony in the Garden* symbolizes comfort and compassion in the midst of suffering. The *Crucifixion* addresses death and grief. *Christ Carried to the Tomb* examines death and acceptance.

At the center of all this is the artist. Still youthful and innocent, he peers at us with eyes half shadowed. The expression is pained, as if he is perplexed by what he comprehends of a complex world in which his role must of necessity be that of participant as well as observer.

Gentle Indignation   **August 1996**

THE ROOF GARDEN AT THE METROPOLITAN MUSEUM

August, 1996

The Highly Opinionated Newsletter

Volume One, Number 12

The Roof Garden at MMA—The view from the Roof Garden at the Metropolitan Museum of Art is over Central Park treetops to the surrounding buildings of the city. It's a wonderful view. The Roof Garden, however, affords few other amenities. Benches around the wall are scarce and when you are seated, the walls obscure the view. While there *is* a refreshment stand, chairs, tables and shade are non-existent. So it's entirely possible to slosh your drink on yourself while sipping it as you stand in the hot sun. The sculpture, meanwhile, is of dubious distinction and may be regarded either as an enhancement, a distraction or an obstruction to the view.

The selection is somewhat odd. It ranges from the representative to the abstract; from the voluptuous to the spare; and from marble to rust to flashy reflective stainless steel. The selection may be regarded either as eclectic or else a mere hodgepodge.

The 1927 Gaston Lachaise bronze *Standing Woman* looks, on closer inspection, as bad as it looks on first. All simpering pulchritude on tip-toe, it is a perfect example of kitsch.

The Lipchitz marble, *Seated Bather* (1927), with its complex design of chiseled semi-circles, has an aesthetic ambiguity.

Even the Rodin *Three Shades* (1881), all rippling musculature, their three bowed heads touching one another in plaintive contrition, appears overly mannered.

A 1965 David Smith stainless steel *Becca* is fabricated of shiny textured metal and resembles a flimsy wooden sawhorse.

A large Tony Smith *Amaryllis* (1965) in black painted steel does have presence. But so would any large L-shaped structure in steel.

Anthony Caro's *Odalisque* (1984) looks playful. Its rusted shapes of industrial wedges and half-circles, its nuts and bolts, made it seem—whether by comparison or default—the most interesting game in town.

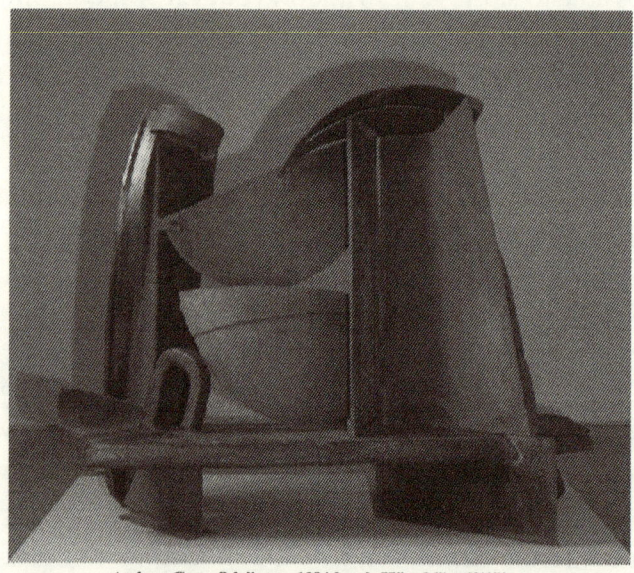

Andrew Caro, Odalisque, 1984 [steel; 77" x 96" x 60½"]

Toulouse-Lautrec at the Metropolitan Museum

August 1996

The Highly Opinionated Newsletter

Volume One, Number 13

Toulouse-Lautrec in the Collection at MMA—Toulouse-Lautrec was attracted to a particular segment of society—the urban demimonde. He was able to enter into this world and to capture its spirit, its activities and its inhabitants with an interest and an intensity entirely his own. Lautrec captured this world with elegance of line, originality of composition, and explosions of color. He never shied away from the strangeness, but embraced and celebrated it instead, leaving a record that even today is startling for its candor and beauty.

But Lautrec's lens was a narrow one, and when focused away from the area he took for his own, the vision was greatly diluted. It is then that the artist's weaknesses appear: the fact that his line lacked the consistent incisiveness of the line of a Daumier, for instance; or that without some strong design element, the work lacks focus. This exhibit, by bringing out a representative sampling of his art, allows us to notice these discrepancies; to see how intimately associated with a single and specific world was the expression of Lautrec's genius.

It is in the posters that Lautrec achieves his greatest work. Composition, line and color fuse, forming unexpected design to which lettering is always integral. This work has power and energy. The 1891 *Moulin Rouge* is divided into foreground, middle and background. In the foreground an odd gray figure gestures toward a woman in a white skirt who dances before a background of onlookers. The slashing red of words, blouse and legs animates the work. In *Aristide Bruant* (1892), it is the jaunty tilt of a hat on an uplifted head and the red of a scarf slung across a cape that give the piece its swagger. In *Jane Avril*, it is the astonishing angle of an upraised leg. And in *Divan Japonais*, it is the elegant curve of black-gloved arms, as well as the outrageous orange of hair and lips. Each work catches, with great elan, the artifice and extravagance of the bohemian milieu.

Oils are generally less effective. Among the exceptions is the 1892 *Englishman of Moulin Rouge*. The leering face of this gentleman, caught between a dark hat and coat and the pale sleeve of a dress, is defined precisely through hue and line. Surely this gentleman is unaware of his own expression and the effect is equally comic and unsettling.

Gouaches and lithographs covering other subject matter seem either too broad or too weak. Caricature often flails. Drawings of the theater are surprisingly bland.

For Lautrec's finest work was inextricably linked to the urban demimonde. This was the world he was drawn to, the world that fascinated and inspired him. It was a world that limited, but also defined his art. At its core, it was flamboyant and sleazy. It was this that intrigued him and it was this that his art so brilliantly transformed.

Gentle Indignation   **August 1996**

Rembrandt at the Morgan Library

October, 1996

The Highly Opinionated Newsletter

Volume One, Number 14

Rembrandt Etchings at the Morgan Library—Somehow, each one of Rembrandt's etchings forms part of a seamless, interconnected whole. From simple portrait to complex biblical scene, from landscape to cottage, the entire work is a single contemplation on the beauty and poignancy, the joys and sorrows—the miracle of human existence.

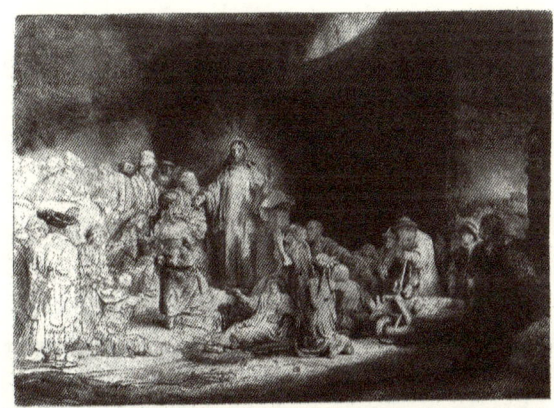

Rembrandt van Rijn, The Hundred Guilder Print (Christ Preaching; Christ Healing the Sick), ca. 1643-49 [etching with drypoint & burin, 2nd state of 2; 11" x 15"]

Exterior incident becomes a gateway to and metaphor of interior states, and the two are seen as inseparable and as one. With exquisite spirituality, the artist composes his theme through painstaking detail. This vision is then worked and reworked. Each successive revisioning heightens the sense of drama and emotion. The separate stages of the etching process allow us to follow the artist, as he searches for and then finds exactly what to eliminate and what to include. As the work unfolds, each piece functions sequentially. Each becomes an occasion in which alternately to express resignation, acceptance, and above all, compassion for the subject—which is always us.

Portraits are a means of examination and self-examination. Individuals from all walks of life are portrayed—artists and merchants, rich and poor. Portraits are fully individualized, yet the feelings expressed are always universal.

Biblical scenes function both literally and metaphorically. Incidents always include the challenges and quests that each of us confronts in life. Abraham becomes a symbol of man seeking guidance and meaning through divine instruction, so faithful that he is willing to undertake any test. Christ embodies the divine among us, an aspect that is both recognized and unrecognized; worshipped and betrayed. *Christ Preaching* (1652) shows the brilliance with which the sacred shines amid the secular. *Three Crosses* (1653) depicts martyrdom, death, finality, and the grieving process. The great *Hundred Guilder Print* (1647–9) represents the divinity that illuminates all of mankind—the shadows that surround us and the beauty that lies within.

Rembrandt never hesitates to rethink work. In *Christ Presented Before the People* (1655), he eliminates a group of onlookers so beautifully delineated that few other artists would either create or choose to eradicate them. But the change is one that simplifies. Likewise, the final state of *Three Crosses* (1653) is a bold revision of the original concept, with slashing lines of darkness now accentuating the drama between human violence and divine love.

Landscapes are spontaneous and invariably touching. Tracts of sky always enfold the abstracted land. Cottages and buildings are dwellings and shelters, which seem to take on the characteristics of unseen inhabitants. *Three Trees* (1643) is worked and reworked so that the contrasting areas of sun and rain expand into a symbolic contrast between darkness and light.

And so the etchings intersect, creating and recreating in their entirety a transcendent world, one that in its wonder and complexity mirrors our own.

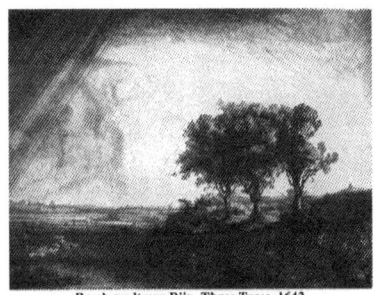

Rembrandt van Rijn, Three Trees, 1643
[etching, drypoint and engraving; 8.4" x 11"]

Gentle Indignation   **October 1996**

DEGAS AT THE ART INSTITUTE OF CHICAGO

October, 1996

The Highly Opinionated Newsletter

Volume One, Number 15

Degas—Beyond Impressionism at the Art Institute of Chicago—
Throughout his life Degas was always exploring, touching everything in
ways that, while connected to traditional art, were somehow brand new.
This included the startlingly off-centered composition, the diffuse color
areas boldly lined to indicate subject matter; and even the choice of
subject matter itself—figures taken from racing, theater, ballet, and
nudes.

It is the thesis of this exhibit that Degas' definitive work occurred
toward the end of his life and so the exhibit brings together pieces from
the later years. But the paucity of major work is evidence that the claim
is unfounded. Later work is looser stylistically, but earlier work is the-
matically related and probably more accomplished. Ironically, then, this
pallid exhibit succeeds best in showing just how wrong its own thesis is.

Early work on view is beautiful. From the moment we see the 1856
Italian Head, with its exquisite draftsmanship and modeling, we recognize a master. The rest of the exhibit is devoted largely to figures from
ballet and to women bathing or grooming.

Ballet pictures are magical. They are about the reality of illusion. They
are about theater as interface between the concrete and the abstract—
the theatrical setting as concrete; the patterning of the performers
within it as abstract. In these paintings, arms and legs are sophisticated

design motifs. Costumes fuse groups of dancers into pools of luminous color. In two lovely early works—the 1874 *Yellow Dancers* and the 1876 *On the Stage* —clusters of dancers delicately frame empty space, a device also used in *Before the Ballet* (1890). In the 1895 *Blue Dancers*, dancers are a whirl of radiant blues.

Ballet pictures are also about the reality *behind* illusion—the arduous preparation or the awkward moment at rehearsal. An 1879 *Three Studies of a Dancer in Fourth Position* beautifully captures a ballet stance as viewed from differing perspectives.

Degas was particularly intrigued with the contradictions of the female—ideal and real, ethereal and earthy, sublime and sensual, intimate and exposed. Sometimes one aspect is explored; at other times, a combination. But always, Degas experiments with the figure —clothed and unclothed; at rest and in motion; weightless and weighted.

Sculpture was used as a study aid as well as an art form. Sculptures are deliberately clumsy and exaggerated, the poses at times almost defying gravity. Surfaces are tactile, displaying the process through which they were built up.

The nude, either in oil or pastel, is rendered in terms of form and flesh, weight and movement. Female bathers range from static to contorted, from raw sketches to fully modeled representations. A 1900–05 *After the Bath* in tones of sepia was quite wonderful. But there were far too many bathers and far too few that were successful.

The series of women combing their hair possess a special and lyrical beauty. The hair, symbol of seduction, has a palpable presence. The large 1892–96 canvas in shimmering reds and pinks is particularly magical.

In the final two galleries were paintings of landscapes and of Russian dancers, not one of which was inspired. Compared with the luminosity of the ballet dancers, the folk dancers seemed coarse and leaden. Blunt landscapes suffered from recollections of delicate monotypes.

The exhibit progressed strangely. The finest works were in the opening galleries. In later galleries, struggle was more visible than achievement. Quantity vastly exceeded quality. As a consequence, there was an abundance of minor work. As occurred with Cézanne in Philadelphia, most decisions made throughout this exhibit served Degas poorly.

Gentle Indignation   **October 1996**

MAX BECKMANN AT THE GUGGENHEIM MUSEUM, SOHO

November, 1996

The Highly Opinionated Newsletter

Volume One, Number 16

Max Beckmann in Exile at the Guggenheim Museum, Soho—Max
Beckmann painted the world he was part of—Germany and World War
II. This was a world totally unhinged, one in which man's inhumanity
to man reached staggering proportions. Beckmann looked at this world
as both participant and observer; victim and witness. He painted its
cruelty and carnage, its pain and suffering. And he transmuted it into a
very personal art.

Beckmann's vocabulary is taken from such places as the carnival, the
circus and the theater. His style is expressionistic and symbolic. Extreme
distortion and heavy black outlines create an effect that seems almost
Biblical at times. Canvases are crammed with figures and crowded with
incident, producing a vision that is both strange and anguished.

Early self-portraits are penetrating and uneasy. They reveal the
charisma of the artist and the facade behind which he is condemned to
hide. Likenesses of the artist appear throughout the work in different
guises, as if to imply that we all have multiple roles.

The 1932 triptych *Departure* incorporates the essential paradoxes of the
human condition through religious imagery drawn from Christianity.
A central panel contains the image of a family—a king, a mother and a
child. They are on a boat, symbolizing the human journey, and are surrounded by the beautiful blue of a serene sky and calm sea. The panels

that flank them contain imagery of the world around them—a world of depravity and cruelty, of bondage and pain. The 1934 *Journey of the Fish* acts as a continuation of and comment upon their journey, as a man and woman plummet from the sky, faces hidden, unmasked through grief.

The 1939 *Bird's Hell* shows how man's role as executioner leads inexorably to the perversion of all nature. In *Acrobats* (1939), we see the infinite human capacity for contortion. How self-destructive our role-playing can be is shown in the powerful triptych *Actors* (1941). Such traits begin with who we are, as shown in *Beginnings* (1946). Again in the 1947 *Air Balloon*, it is by our own nature that we are bounded and caged. *Rescue* (1948) shows a worn-out man and woman, barely surviving in a raft barely large enough to support them. *Blind Man's Buff* (1944) shows—through the call of music and the feeble light of a candle—the life of the spirit from which man turns away.

The 1950 *Falling Man* is about expulsion, man's descent from grace. The 1950 triptych *Argonauts* is about a quest for meaning, sometimes of the senses, at other times of the soul.

And so Beckmann records, with outrage and with irony, the blood dripping from the human experience. He records the tensions existing between man and man and man and woman. But every now and then, amid the carnage of our race, he finds some small solace, some faint glimmer of hope.

Gentle Indignation   **November 1996**

GALLERIES AT 57TH STREET

November, 1996

The Highly Opinionated Newsletter

Volume One, Number 17

Galleries at 57th Street—Prowling the galleries around 57th Street served only to reinforce my sense of the paltry nature of much of what passes for art in this century.

I began at Janis Gallery, where stepping off the elevator, the first thing I encountered was a frightening electric-blue spongelike fungus shape clinging to the wall. I was taken aback. Stunned would be too mild too describe my reaction. I glanced quickly around the premises and saw that no names were attached to any of the work. Putting aside for the moment the crazy idea that no artist cared to be associated with anything on display, I went up to the desk to ask for a title list. "Most of our customers recognize these artists without needing a list," the woman in charge icily informed me. I was utterly undeterred. "Sometimes I just like to know what the title is," I parried. She dismissively handed me the list on condition that I would promise to return it. Unable to think of anything better to do with it anyway, I promised.

Numbered list in hand, I thought I would check out the work, only to discover that they were unnumbered. An inquiry to a young man working in the gallery elicited the information that he didn't know any more than I did. Together, we tried to figure out a probable order.

It really didn't matter. Nothing was as horrific as the blue spongelike fungus by Yves Klein, but nothing was much better, either. Several small

Giacometti drawings did exert an accustomed spell. A Brancusi oval entitled *Prometheus* looked like all his other ovals given other titles like *Muse* or *Woman Sleeping* or *Child*. The usual array of abstractions was looking tired and familiar and also rather hackneyed. By the time I got to the DuChamp urinal, pointless though it was, it was looking pretty good. In fact, it seemed like the high point of this selection. In such company, a little wit goes a long way.

Edwin Dickinson at Babcock—Drawings of nudes had authority as well as delicacy. Landscapes were introspective in quality, muted in color. Easy to look at, easy to forget.

Eric Fischl at Mary Boone—These eerie and erotically charged paintings stay in your mind because of an unlikely combination. They are bad as well as weird.

Ellsworth Kelly at Sheehan—With sheet after sheet of nothing more than a single color, this artist's work appears monotonous, repetitious, and just plain boring.

Works at O'Hara and at Goodman—Twentieth century work begins to be too assaultive and aggressive to spend much time with. A childish Basquiat that would be embarrassing anywhere seems even more so on a gallery wall. Botero's blimplike women are creatures you want to flee from as soon as you can. A Matta is filled with unpleasant looming shapes. I had never seen an ugly Brancusi, but here it was—a gouache, poorly painted and ugly, too. Et cetera.

Gentle Indignation   **November 1996**

Corot at the Metropolitan Museum

November, 1996

The Highly Opinionated Newsletter

Volume One, Number 18

Corot at MMA—Corot was a gifted painter, poised between two eras. He turned his attention primarily to landscape painting, and here he had at his service a large technique and an even larger sense of nostalgia. The landscape paintings for which he is best known are romantic, decorative and backward-looking. Many are of imaginary places filled with mythological creatures cavorting in idyllic shaded glades. Content may be close to banal, but technique always retains an alluring poetry. Small landscapes are fluid and loose, focusing on mood and atmosphere in ways that anticipate the Impressionist movement to come. The major surprise of the exhibit was the portraits of women. Stolid, monumental and unadorned, they have a reality and an honesty that the landscapes lack. These women, caught almost unaware, have a simple dignity that gives them impact and presence. With their sense of inner strength, they look forward to women of the twentieth century.

Earliest landscapes are of actual places and are exploratory. Color is applied broadly, glossing over detail and bringing out shape and shadow. The 1830 *Honfleur Fishing Boat*, with its palette of blue, ochre and black, seems like a harbinger of later Manet. There is a freshness to the sweep of panoramic vistas and, in the more confined settings, there is a liveliness in the patterned play of sunlight.

But as the artist embarks on larger, more ambitious work, a different vision emerges—one based upon place as an idealized surrounding.

Large shadowy landscapes provide an idyllic setting in which mythological stories are enacted and Arcadian fantasies take place. While sections of the landscape are brushed in with extraordinary beauty, as a whole these landscapes look overstated and embarrassing to twentieth century tastes. The large and crowded 1838 *Silenus* seems particularly contrived and silly. Figured works accepted into the prestigious French salon seem weak and superficial as well.

Against these canvases, portraits from the 50's to the 70's stand out in every way. Instead of the idealized, there is the real. Instead of the sentimentalized, there is the honest. A surprising beauty based on the commonplace appears. The three versions of *Artist's Studio* (1865–70) are touching in simplicity and intimacy of vision. And every woman—however ordinary the activity she is engaged in—possesses stature and meaning. *Greek Girl* (1872), delicious in whites, seems to pause for a moment, lost in thought.

Lady in Blue (1874) is wonderfully complex—simultaneously strong and gentle, alert and in repose. The head is delicate, the arms large, the dress a sweep in blue. *Monk with Cello* (1874) is an isolated figure who retreats from an outer world into a world of music.

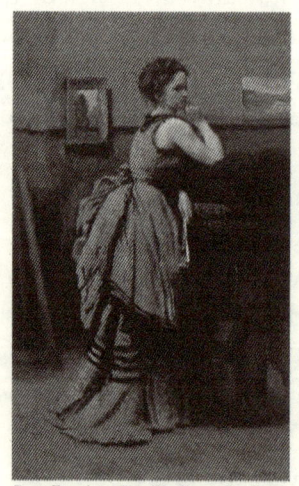

A mysterious *Moonlit Landscape* (1874) is a mass of lush dark foliage surrounding a pale blue oval of sky and sea.

And so Corot is an artist of great contrast, with work ranging from the overly sentimental and ornate to work of quiet grandeur. He considered it his mission "to

Jean-Baptiste-Camille Corot, La Dame en bleu (Lady in Blue), 1874 [oil on canvas; 31½" x 19?"]

make landscapes." And he did. But ironically, his finest work may have been the women he saw no need to embellish. In allowing them to speak for themselves, he endowed them with the power to speak eloquently.

Gentle Indignation   **November 1996**

Jasper Johns at the Museum of Modern Art

November, 1996

The Highly Opinionated Newsletter

Volume One, Number 19

Jasper Johns at MOMA—Johns' surfaces are seductive. Few artists are able to design work as handsome and exuberant, using elements as ordinary as letters, numbers and varied symbols of Americana. Separated from their accustomed context, these elements assume a new personality. They acquire almost mythic dimension. They draw one in. It is only later that one begins to wonder about the immediacy of the impact, and to notice that, upon repeated viewing, the impact diminishes. One starts to wonder about the process that has gone into this art—and to wonder whether this process can transform symbols taken from the vernacular into high art. Or whether this attempt, provocative though it may be, is merely clever.

Johns' prints are beautifully crafted. First, a theme is set out in a realistic way, with subsequent variations becoming progressively more abstract. The prints can be seen as visual mind games—a way of deconstructing image, word and letter. The series *After Holbein* deconstructs a portrait in seven different ways, ultimately reducing it to a series of design.

The paintings take familiar images and by recontextualizing them, attempt to transform them in much the same way as DuChamp attempted to recontextualize and transform ready-made objects. The paintings of the 60's are large and lush. Color, texture and design are dazzling. There is no doubt that Johns is master of his craft. And of deception. Flags, bulls-eyes, numbers, letters, words—all undergo deft metamorphosis. They are shifted and distorted until, barely recognizable, they acquire a strange beauty. But is this beauty only surface deep? Is it merely shallow? Unfortunately, one suspects so.

The 70's were an excursion into total abstraction. But the artist seemed uncomfortable and the excursion had virtually nowhere to go. Color is garish, shape is awkward, and when constructions are added, they seem to be mere gimmicks in an unsuccessful attempt to get something going. From the 80's on, the artist recycles his own material. But as he does so, the material becomes trivial and stale. By 1988, he tries pop imagery. However, this imagery is simplified to the point of embarrassment. Among the worst examples are the hideous eye-balls afloat in neon color fields. Johns seems to be looking for some new vocabulary and to be hopelessly lost.

In 1986, however, in the *Seasons* paintings, this search briefly took on a lyrical quality that is quite touching. Here, the artist's own simple gray silhouette haunts each canvas and each canvas alludes to a cycle in life. The work is both autobiographical and elegiac. There are problems, but the artist is showing vulnerability. This work may be as deep—and as good—as Johns gets.

Gentle Indignation   **November 1996**

THE PAULA COOPER GALLERY, CHELSEA

November, 1996

The Highly Opinionated Newsletter

Volume One, Number 20

The Paula Cooper Gallery—Does the Paula Cooper Gallery's move to 20th Street and 10th Avenue signal the demise of twentieth century American art?

The gallery is in a location that no one goes to. The door is marked so discretely that it is easily missed. Entry is difficult. And what passes for art could be a joke if it weren't so depressing. The small number of people rotated in and out as quickly as if they were using a revolving door.

Among the objects on view, if that is what it can be called, were a number of empty soda bottles strung together; a butter churn; and a large white Styrofoam funnel. A second room held a series of nineteen bad sketches of three steps. Also a series of crude drawings of the head of a giraffe licking something that might be a stanchion. Or might not. It really didn't matter.

There was nothing of interest on any level. Was this art or non-art? What about content or technique? Let alone an idea or an aesthetic? I could only exit as quickly as possible and try to contain my dismay.

The ghost of Marcel DuChamp seems to be everywhere. Is this DuChamp's final revenge against the art world he mocked? An art world which now embraces his mockery. And an art that now incorporates his anti-aesthetics. Perhaps this is his ultimate irony. If so, it is an irony which had already worn stale during DuChamp's own tenure.

Being an optimist, I would like to think that the New York art scene has nowhere to go but up. But experience tells me that such optimism is likely to prove wrong.

Gentle Indignation   **November 1996**

Volume Two

Tiepolo at the Morgan Library

April, 1997

The Highly Opinionated Newsletter

Volume Two, Number 1

Tiepolo at the Morgan Library—Through virtuoso drawing, Giambattista Tiepolo invites us into realms of fantasy, religious and mythological domains. Scenes are composed through lively line and skillful washes of lights and darks.

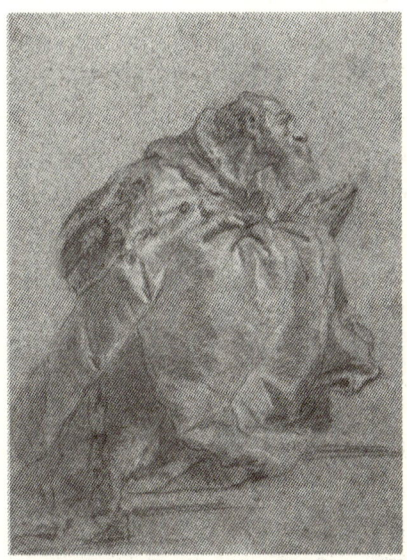

Giovanni Battista Tiepolo, A King Kneeling, c. 1753 [red chalk heightened with white on blue-gray paper; 31.2" x 22.5"]

Unfortunately, many of the drawings tend to be ornate. Too much is going on and too many figures are competing for attention. Action lacks a focal point. Embellishments are distracting. As a consequence, the story line is frequently both diffuse and confusing. And the elaborate representation becomes decorative.

Early drawings—from 1715 to 1735—can show occasional anatomical inaccuracies. In a drawing of *Hercules*, one leg is too short. In work such as *Angels*, *Nude Man Seated* and *St. Andrew*, arms on figures are uneven in length. Surprisingly awkward decisions are made, as when all that is visible of the kneeling figure of Abraham is his rear end.

From 1735 onward, Tiepolo's work is at its strongest. Drawings are abundant but also complex. Those that stand out do so through their simplicity. In one of five *Annunciations,* two lovely figures communicate with a direct spareness. *Study for Oval Ceiling* has an abstract spontaneity. Three studies of *St. Patrick* are studies in fluidity of line. Two small religious scenes—*Hagar and Ishmael* and *Flight Into Egypt*—are rather touching. And in *Holy Family Under a Tree*, the three figures merge into a graceful unit.

Several studies of heads drawn in red chalk are also powerfully rendered. In three—*Man with Mustache and Turban, Bearded Man* and *Giulio Contrini*—lines display endless invention.

But the overall impression of Tiepolo's work is unrestrained exuberance. The effect can be stifling. Occasionally among the excesses, something modest appears. When that happens, the effect is as bracing as a breeze of fresh air.

Gentle Indignation   **April 1997**

TRASHING SOHO

April, 1997

The Highly Opinionated Newsletter

Volume Two, Number 2

Special Issue: Trashing Soho—The phrase "trashing Soho" is intended as a pejorative. But in a place where trash is in and even encouraged, it is alas! sadly descriptive. Indeed, it is a sad commentary on any culture when such a description tells what's happening. And spending time in Soho can indeed be a dismaying experience.

Among recent exhibits, the following demonstrate both the glaring weaknesses and tenuous strengths of what always seems to be a frantic quest for something completely different.

Jessica Stockholder at Jay Gorney—OMITTED

Miriam Schapiro at Steinbaum-Krauss—OMITTED

Roxy Paine at Ronald Feldman—Experimentation for the sake of experimentation continues. Objects are all over the floor and range from something that looks like a white plaster circuit board to representations of fields of mushrooms and poison ivy. A computer controlled board drips white latex paint. Get it? The computer makes art by and for the artist. But visually, there is no point to any of it. And it is all conceptually trite.

Intimate Universe at Steele—A group of about seventy small canvases show, in about seventy different ways, how little is going on in either abstraction or representation. Ideas that were pallid to begin with are recycled and become even more pallid. Here and there an exception occurs, as with Joan Nelson's lovely landscapes employing Renaissance motifs. We are grateful for anything that stands apart from the general mediocrity of vision and technique.

June Leaf at Edward Thorp—Ms. Leaf's works combine tin, paper mache and painted canvas. A solitary figure constructed of soldered tin is usually small in scale and juxtaposed against a painted background. The effect is often arresting and is enhanced by titles which impart a grand sweep to the work. However the work can tend toward the melo-dramatic. And a muddy palette and intentionally awkward technique on the canvas don't contribute much. But all in all this work displays a rare sense of integrity.

Gentle Indignation   **April 1997**

CHINESE ART GALLERIES AT THE METROPOLITAN MUSEUM

May, 1997

The Highly Opinionated Newsletter

Volume Two, Number 3

Chinese Art Galleries at MMA—The newly installed Chinese Art galleries provide a glorious respite from our chaotic art scene. Twentieth century disorder cedes to timeless order here. Pointlessness and pain cede to the tranquil and the transcendent. Art retreats from a world askew and ascends to a different plane. And we ascend to that level, too, as we contemplate intimations of a far higher, more meaningful realm than the one we are accustomed to inhabit.

Our first glimpse of the magnificent Southern Tang drawing *Riverbank* sweeps us into this realm. Lofty mountains lift in subtle arcs to unknown, unknowable heights. The Northern Sung *Summer Mountains* by Qu Ding positions these same elements in a horizontal context. The composition, with its long flowing river, evokes the vastness and majesty of an environment of which we are part. In *Old Trees, Level Distance* by Guo Xi, atmospheric effects isolate every element. Here and there a

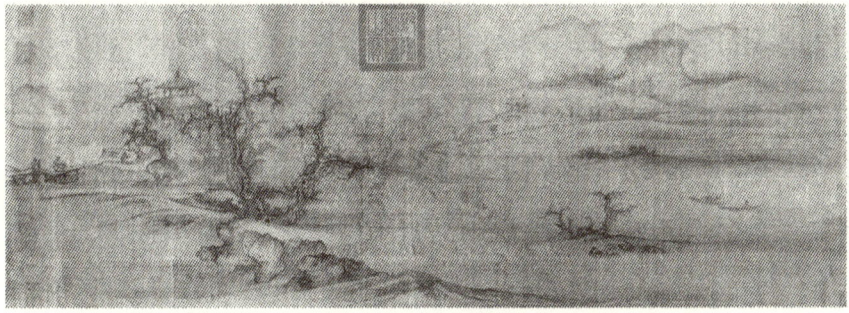

Guo Xi, Old Trees, Level Distance, ca. 1000–ca. 1090 [handscroll; ink and color on silk; 13 3/4" x 41 ¼"]

mountain, a tree, a bridge, a house, boats, and toiling figures emerge. The entire panorama suggests nothing so much as the individual life journey, with its alternating experiences of sadness and of beauty.

The Southern Song's aesthetic is a highly selective one. Every element acquires philosophical connotation. Every element becomes symbolic of the whole. The whole becomes a contemplation on the mystery of the universe and of man's place in it. The cosmos is seen as paradoxical in nature. Though an inscrutable void, its emptiness forms everything. In each work, form and content merge with exquisite clarity and distillation.

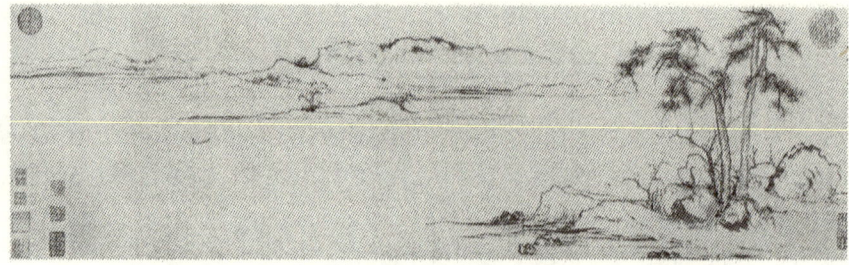

Zhao Mengfu, Twin Pines, Level Distance [detail], c.1300 [handscroll: ink on paper; 10.5"x 42.2"]

The Song period represents for me the height of Chinese artistic achievement. Soon thereafter, refinement of technique and of outlook diminishes. Work throughout the Yuan Dynasty is marked by increased solidity and less fluidity; increased coarseness and less transcendence. Of all the work on view from this period, only *Twin Pines, Level Distance* by Zhao Mengfu depicts the landscape in a way that still has imprints of a former beauty.

With the fifteenth and sixteenth centuries, refinement of composition diminishes even more. Color intrudes in a decorative manner. Heaviness weighs the landscape down. These trends continue throughout the Qing Dynasty (1644–1911). Unattractive shapes form unattractive patterns, often crowding the picture plane and eliminating a sense of space or vastness. Nature can be threatening, at times even sinister. One exception is *Misty Bamboo on a Distant Mountain* (1753) by Zheng Xie. Here, the bamboo creates an overall pattern of delicate rhythmic abstraction.

What the twentieth century will produce is still to be assessed. Western influence abounds. In Fu Baoshi's *Playing Weiqi at the Water Pavilion*, humor and action combine with expressionistic aspects in a new and playful way. But China's past has reached artistic heights that provide so much upon which to draw. How does an artist select from so rich a source? This problem is one faced repeatedly by every artist in every culture. The future remains an open experiment.

Gentle Indignation   **May 1997**

Rodin and Michelangelo at the Philadelphia Museum of Art

May, 1997

The Highly Opinionated Newsletter

Volume Two, Number 4

Rodin and Michelangelo at the Philadelphia Museum of Art—Rodin may have been greatly influenced by Michelangelo, but this exhibit makes a sad and curious conjunction. Every comparison does Rodin a disservice. Michelangelo defined sculpture for all time. His signature is indelible and inimitable. No sculptor can withstand comparison. Nor should any. Each sculptor must stand upon a body of work that reflects a vision so unique that none but he could have created it. When this exhibit allows Rodin to be Rodin, this occurs. When it does not, it undercuts both Rodin's achievement and our response to it.

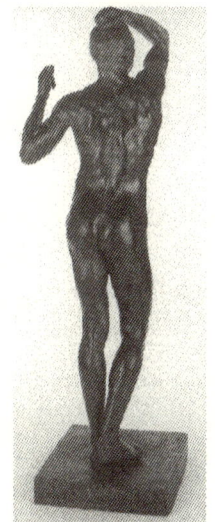

Michelangelo, Male Nude Viewed from the Back, c.1504-5 [pen and ink on paper; 16 1/16" x 11 3/16"]

The opening galleries confuse issues of individuality and identity. Rodin's early *Age of Bronze* and his famous *Thinker* stand in jarring contrast with a replica of Michelangelo's late

Auguste Rodin,
The Age of Bronze, 1875-76
[bronze; height 67"]

mannerist statues from the Medici Tomb. Each work seems isolated in its own space and fails to relate to any of the others.

Confusion continues in the next gallery. Very little structure or coherence is apparent. Sculpture and drawing seem haphazardly placed. Occasionally, amid the disorder, a piece reaches out. If so, it is always a piece by Michelangelo: two superb small *River God* torsos left unfinished; sketches of torsos, legs, arms. Each piece is a powerful exploration of anatomy and musculature, of motion and tension in balance. Each piece displays a large and restless intelligence, a questing imagination. The beauty stuns. Michelangelo's drawings *Libyan Sibyl* (1511) and *Male Nude Viewed from the Back* (1584), two of the most remarkable studies ever created, blaze forth like laser beams.

Whatever Rodin undertakes is diminished by the comparison. Or, worse still, is made to seem melodramatic. This happens especially with Rodin's *The Call to Arms* (1879) and *I Am Beautiful* (1882), two strange sculptures whose excesses appear all the more exaggerated in this context.

It is only when Michelangelo is left behind that Rodin has a chance to stand on his own merits. And in a gallery devoted solely to Rodin, those merits are visible. They are there in the quiet stance and gesture of *Sant John the Baptist Preaching* (1878). And in the wonderful interplay of the hand sculptures. These sculptures depict a large array of human emotion and activity—including intuition and reflection; tension and ease; faith and creativity. *Hand of God* (1898) and *Hand of Rodin Holding a Torso* (1917) both evoke the miracle and the mystery of creation, an inexplicable act that produces something from nothing.

Two poles of human experience—poignancy and power—are embodied in *Study for Eustace de St. Pierre* (1886) and *Balzac 'F' Athlete* (1896). The former figure is a solitary one—lean, muscular and vulnerable. In the latter, the torso becomes a terrain of coiled tension and might.

And so Rodin is allowed to come into his own. Faults remain. Far too much is theatrical and sentimental. But when his particular strengths speak out they do so with distinction and with eloquence.

Gentle Indignation   **May 1997**

THE BARNES COLLECTION
(PHILADELPHIA)

June, 1997

The Highly Opinionated Newsletter

Volume Two, Number 5

The Barnes Collection Philadelphia—Depending upon one's tolerance for eccentricity, visiting the Barnes Collection can be merely exasperating or else an ordeal. The collection is highly eccentric in terms both of its content and how it is hung. The rare masterpiece is surrounded by quantities of mediocre work. Everything is so tightly packed together that viewing is difficult. Adding to the visual clutter are dark metal ornaments that dot the wall wherever a vacancy might otherwise occur.

The collection is characterized by a lack of either specific or definitive vision. The resulting eclecticism is confusing. The collection becomes an artistic grab bag, as lesser works contend with and distract from those that are superior. Absent entirely is a sense of the exhilaration generated by a careful selectivity of mind and eye.

Renoirs appear throughout the collection almost like a leit-motif. Large fleshy nudes flash acres of soft candy-colored skin in treacly profusion. The nudes soon seem repetitious and formulaic. As the figures become inflated to seemingly gargantuan proportions, they also become grotesque. But they are all around and cannot be avoided.

Nonetheless, the presence of Cézanne, Picasso and Matisse is reason enough that the Barnes Collection should be seen. As is one extraordinary Seurat.

Seurat's *Models* is a large canvas in which a single figure is represented in three different poses. It is, for me, this artist's finest work. Simplicity and grace suffuse the entire piece, which is both testament and tribute to the beauty of the female form.

The Matisses are wonderful, as well. In the glorious *Blue Still Life*, warm tones of fruit are placed against a cool patterned setting in such a way that the subject matter vanishes, transformed into a scintillating field of radiant color. The *Seated Odalisque*, too, dissolves into a series of patterned color. The *Dance* murals consist of flattened figures that flit in silhouette against semi-circular arches.

Then there are the Picassos. The tender representational early work predominates. In the main gallery, *Peasants* has an authoritative elegance in its over-all design. Elsewhere, in a small piece, a youth is poised tremulously on the threshold of experience. In *Acrobat* and *Young Harlequin*, two exotic figures stand linked yet isolated, posed against a dream-like background.

Numerous Cézannes are scattered throughout. They range through portraits, landscapes and still-lifes. The portraits are as enigmatic as always. Landscapes, while fine, are better realized elsewhere. The still-lifes are powerful metaphors in geometry for the ordered sensuality of nature. But Cézanne's work benefits from being seen together and because it is not, its power is diminished.

A room filled with drawings contains wonderful examples of Goya, Cézanne and Picasso. But these, too, may be easily overlooked because they are cramped by crowded surroundings.

So here, as throughout the Barnes collection, while much patience is necessary, such patience is also greatly rewarded.

Gentle Indignation   **June 1997**

MATISSE AND TERIADE AT THE YOSHII GALLERY

July, 1997

The Highly Opinionated Newsletter

Volume Two, Number 6

Matisse and Teriade at Yoshii Gallery—This exhibit is about the collaboration between the artist and the publisher Teriade. Works on paper appear along with preliminary studies. The artist abstracts from reality in such a way that simple elements become designs and motifs. A joyous exuberance is everywhere. Work looks as though it has simply sprung to life. The surprising discovery is that it both has and hasn't.

Extensive studies provide a glimpse of the artistic process. They also show the amount of preparation involved, as the artist works and reworks themes. Always present is a glow of excitement and a sense of exploration and discovery.

Nothing escapes Matisse's vision. He will take anything and everything for his subject matter. Letters of the alphabet are repeated until they become swirls of design. Familiar shapes of circles, stars and hearts shift ever so slightly to become new and unfamiliar. Grillwork and other ornamentation fill the pages like odd hieroglyphics. Flowers and leaves assume delicately sensual outline. Lines flow succulently as they delineate fruit. Other lines swoop to indicate the female form. Rows of nun's faces—alike in their fullness of faith—are somehow still sweetly individualized.

Many of these elements combine in the books. Pages practically burst with joyous illustration. Covers explore the myriad ways in which the medium of color and composition may relate the message. The title, *VERVE*, is played with. The word is disassembled and broken into constituent and intriguing parts. Figures cavort in varying positions among these letters and against varied fields of varied leaves. Content and form merge into an overall pattern. There is a sense everywhere of abundance and of profusion.

And of joy. Especially joy. Of the joy underlying the realm of the physical, the realm of the senses and the realm of the spiritual. Of a transcendent connection between everything that exists. Of movement and change. Of darkness and of light. And of celebration.

For Matisse sees life as an occasion to celebrate. And to everything he sees, Matisse has one instinct. The instinct to affirm.

Gentle Indignation   **July 1997**

"Objects of Desire" at the Museum of Modern Art

August, 1997

The Highly Opinionated Newsletter

Volume Two, Number 7

"Objects of Desire" at the Museum of Modern Art—This still life exhibit manages to convince us, no matter how hard it tries to prove otherwise, that there is still no life in much new work. The new work consists of objects instead of art. A long tradition that had allowed for the highest expression of technique and vision is being replaced. As we proceed through the galleries, we see art vanish chronologically. Gimmickry in the name of innovation appears instead. The words "still life" revert to their literal French origin. "Nature morte." A wonderful tradition is dead and dying.

The exhibit is divided into nine sections. Each has a title as pretentious and tendentious as the title of the exhibit.
The meaning of that title completely eludes me. The more so as I find the objects so far from desirable as to be rather repugnant.

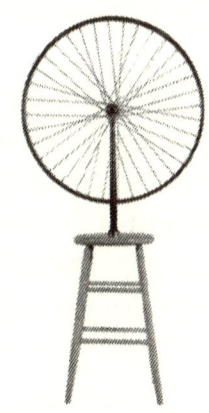

The art of painting remains very much alive early in the show. A lovely Cézanne *Still Life With Ginger Jar* (1890) hangs at the entry to the exhibit. It is a poignant reminder of the great tradition of which it

Marcel DuChamp, Bicycle Wheel, 1951 (after lost original of 1913) [assemblage; metal wheel mounted on painted wooden stool; 50½" x 25½" x 16 5/8"]

is part, a tradition which this show does much to attempt to eradicate. As such, it appears even more vulnerable.

Canvases by Matisse shine with clarity of color and intricacy of design. *Purple Cyclamen* (1911–13) and *Apples* (1916) splash color and design with exuberance. The work of Picasso and Braque play with perception. Picasso's *Guitar* (1912), sculpted of metal and wire, is a winsome exploration of space. Klee's private vocabulary ushers us into the imaginary world he creates. Cornell builds small boxes that allude to such large matters as the role of order and disorder in the world and in art. In all, this work delights.

But with Marcel DuChamp, represented here by the 1951 *Bicycle Wheel*, a fundamental change occurs in twentieth century art. Now any object becomes art whenever a recognized artist says it is. And the less it is touched by the the hand of the artist, the better. Art as discipline cedes to art as anything. Or art as nothing. For nearly fifty years, this philosophy has captivated and enthralled an entire art world. The philosophy is anti-art. And it has long since lost whatever wit and novelty it may once have had.

Pop art borrows from commercial technique and takes everyday items as its subject matter. Art now loses its fine art quality and acquires a banality which never transforms or transcends the subject. The banal remains just that. Banal. Campbell's Soup, Brillo Boxes, Spam, Keds. Brand names proliferate as if advertisement and art were one. Even trash is treated as if it were art. Or as if art were trash. Or merited being treated as such. It all seems as tiresome as it does pointless.

The final section entitled Postmodern is the final indignity. Still life declines into lurid photos of food, food itself, and kitchen objects so enlarged in scale as to acquire through size an effect they lack through quality. As does much of modern art. A marble slab containing a barely visible layer of milk is set into an altar-like space. It provides an unintentional metaphor for the sorry direction the entire enterprise has taken. It is as if the venerable Museum of Modern Art were worshipping at an empty altar.

This altar contains absolutely nothing. And they don't know it.

Gentle Indignation   **August 1997**

STEIGLITZ AT THE
METROPOLITAN MUSEUM

August, 1997

The Highly Opinionated Newsletter

Volume Two, Number 8

Stieglitz at the Metropolitan Museum of Art—These photographs of Georgia O' Keeffe form a pictorial essay of stages of her life as woman and as artist. The subject matter ranges through portraits and nudes to studies of hands. The work is predominantly in glossy black and white and the lighting is at once dramatic and harsh. Theatrical contrasts recall the unnatural lighting effects of a Caravaggio canvas or a Mappelthorpe photograph.

The expression of O'Keeffe's face is frequently mask-like, even blank. O'Keeffe appears to be a woman who does not want to make herself easily known. Nor does she make us want to know her.

The nude torso is examined with a detachment that can seem clinical, in a way that can seem confrontational and aggressive. Because of this, these nudes can appear as voyeuristic as they do artistic. Only in the subtler silvertone prints does a tender quality that is otherwise lacking appear.

Stieglitz is best known for the photographs of O'Keeffe's hands. The hands are posed carefully for maximum effect. They float against their dark background as if disembodied. Gesture is exaggerated and contrived. Stark lighting makes these real hands seem almost unreal. But when compared with the small hands sculpted by Rodin, these hands seem staged. Even showy. These hands seem to be more about artifice than about art.

I had expected something quite different from the Stieglitz photos. Something subtler, deeper and more sincere. Too often it appeared as if the photographer and his subject were at odds. As if Stieglitz needed to exert total control; to manipulate. And as if O'Keeffe, aware of this tendency, deeply resented and resisted it.

In addition, I came away with a sense that the work was self-conscious and artsy. And that the entire art scene of which Stieglitz was part must have fostered and rewarded such traits.

And, too, I came away from the exhibit as I frequently do after viewing work of O'Keeffe. I came away liking her a little bit less than I had before.

Gentle Indignation   **August 1997**

BYZANTIUM AT SINAII AT THE METROPOLITAN MUSEUM

August, 1997

The Highly Opinionated Newsletter

Volume Two, Number 9

Byzantium at Sinaii at MMA—Previously part of a much larger Byzantium exhibit, these twelve pieces are on loan from a monastery in Egypt. They are small in scale, illustrational in content and symbolic in nature. They are part of a long religious tradition. As such, they minimize innovation and maximize spiritual teaching through parable. Because they rely so much upon religious and artistic convention, they are highly stylized and conventional.

In contrast to twentieth century values, Byzantine art favors stability of content over exploration of form. Both content and form are set according to tradition. The message is the medium, and not the other way around. Using religious metaphor, the work speaks plainly and quietly about the human predicament. But it does so in ways that are so repetititious as to start to seem bland.

The 12th century *Heavenly Ladder* is a gold field patterned with small figures against a diagonal ladder. Both *Moses at the Burning Bush* and *Liturgical Homilies* are intimate and refined. The *Icon with St. Nicholas*, from the 10th to 11th century, depicts a contemplative head with modeling so beautiful that it almost prefigures qualities we associate with later Renaissance developments.

Throughout these works, the religious—never the secular—dominates. The religious imparts what meaning there may be. But it then restricts what form the expression may take. Convention provides a common artistic language. But then it circumscribes it.

The religious context, therefore, provides both strength and weakness. It provides a strong spiritual element that is missing from contemporary work. But it stifles artistic possibilities so severely that a sameness wraps one work after another like a pall.

Gentle Indignation   **August 1997**

DEGAS AT THE METROPOLITAN MUSEUM

October, 1997

The Highly Opinionated Newsletter

Volume Two, Number 10

Degas' Collection at MMA—Degas' collection is astonishing in scope, both in terms of size and content. The collection is large and encompasses a range of artists. But what is unusual is the number of pieces which show these artists at their best.

The museum exhibition seems to set two goals. The first is to display the extraordinary quality of the Degas collection. The second is to show how his collection relates to his work. Although the collection would have benefited from editing, the exhibition meets the first goal admirably. But the second goal is more difficult and here the exhibition falters. The Degas work on view is comparatively weak. We never really see the magnitude of what he accomplished. And the wonderful connection between influence and achievement is left largely unexplored.

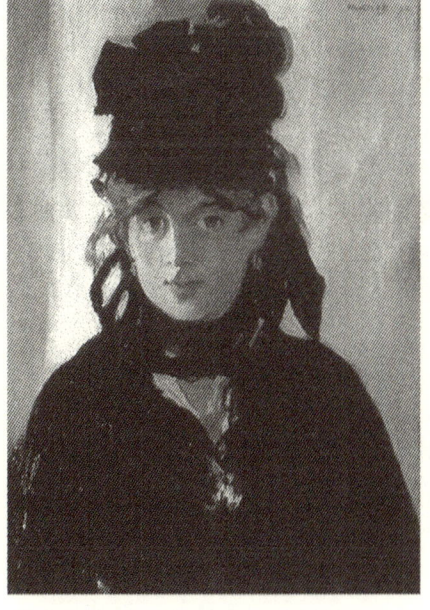

Edouard Manet, Berthe Morisot with a Bunch of Violets, 1872 [oil on canvas; 21½" x 15"]

Both Ingres and Delacroix were of great importance to Degas. In a way, they complement each other. Ingres' work possesses a linear beauty and solidity of mass. There is a sense of containment and refinement that imparts an overall quiet and static quality. This same quality is seen in early Degas. Delacroix' work, on the other hand, is far more dynamic in shape and color. This greater freedom, likewise, gradually appears in later Degas.

Daumier's work is as wonderful as always in its wit and vitality. An artist named Gavarni makes an unlikely and extensive appearance. His work is well-crafted but illustrational. What it meant for Degas we can only ponder.

The Impressionists are well represented. Manet drawings are bold. Among these, certainly the most beautiful is the 1872 head of *Berthe Morisot*, with delicate features lushly framed in blacks. Etchings of Cassatt and Pissarro are not particularly distinguished. Gauguin oils are. Among his many fine canvases, *Woman of the Mango* (1892), with its unexpected and vibrant colors, stands out. An 1887 *Two Sunflowers* by Van Gogh is an abstract swirl of strokes. Each Cézanne is exquisite. The 1888 *Three Pears* has a delicate translucency. The 1877 *V. Choquet* is portrait as landscape. There are lovely oils by Pissarro and Sisley.

The Degas drawings are equal in beauty to anything in the show. My own favorites were *Seated Dancer Tying Her Slipper* (1876), the posture startlingly symmetrical and breathtakingly abstract; *Factory Smoke* (1876), a little monotype in which the intangible is caught; and *Nude Woman Standing Drying Herself* (1891), with its seductively tilted figure and shapely buttock.

But the selection of Degas oils was quite disappointing. The finest works on view were the *Belleli Family* (1858–67) and *Jacques Tissot*

(1867). But these are works that illustrate Degas' firm foundation in the past. They provide wonderful examples of where he came from. But they provide little indication of where he would go. They do not show the subject matter he would take for his own. Nor the astonishing techniques he would come to explore.

And so Degas' own work ironically constitutes the major weakness of the show. It fails to generate the very sense of discovery and excitement that viewing much of his collection had provided. For an artist of Degas' stature, this is inexcusable.

Gentle Indignation   **October 1997**

SCHIELE AT THE MUSEUM OF MODERN ART

October, 1997

The Highly Opinionated Newsletter

Volume Two, Number 11

Egon Schiele at MOMA—To say that Egon Schiele's work is strange is an understatement. His concern with the figure is an excursion into the bizarre. Everything bears the mark of psychic unease. The flesh is seen as a source of continual pain. The body is portrayed as a container of angst and humiliation. There is a self obsession that somehow minimizes self. An obsession with genitalia that somehow vulgarizes sex. Each person is subjected to a process of depersonification, remaining trapped forever inside a body he cannot escape.

Distortion is everywhere, conveyed with great linear facility. Nervous energy and tension erupt throughout. The body undergoes startling angular contortions. The familiar becomes unfamiliar. Subject becomes object. Everything exists in a kind of imbalance. Outer imbalance serves as a mirror for inner imbalance.

The single tender portrait in the exhibit is the 1906 *Portrait of a Young Girl*. In his 1910 *Self Portrait*, the artist stares at us uncomfortably. He is coyly aware of viewing the viewer viewing him. In the 1911 *Draped Self Portrait*, Schiele portrays himself as skeletal as an image of death.

Most of the drawings are of female figures with skirts raised to show explicit and exaggerated genitals. Identity resides in these sexual organs. Exposure is blatant, aggressive and painful. Such exposure defines as well as diminishes the subject. The prurient quality is one equally of fascination and repulsion.

The cumulative impression of the work resembles nothing so much as a kind of tabloid artistry. It is ultimately reductive. We are seen as incapable of transcending our most hapless impulses. We are victimized by our desperate need for sensual pleasures which are invariably accompanied by psychic pain.

Schiele's world is a world of agony without ecstasy. Of alienation and helplessness without courage or hope. It is a world devoid of love or tenderness, in which ours is a nature that lacks grace. His is a dire view of the human condition. A view that is as disturbed as it is disturbing.

Gentle Indignation   **October 1997**

Diebenkorn at the Whitney

October, 1997

The Highly Opinionated Newsletter

Volume Two, Number 12

Richard Diebenkorn at the Whitney—The Whitney retrospective traces the artist's career from its beginning, as he explores the idioms of abstraction, through his foray into figurative art, then back again as he returns to abstraction. We come to admire the impulses that the artist obeyed as time and again he changed course. We come to understand some of the elements he wished to incorporate or to eliminate in his ongoing quest to refine his vision. We see the artists who influenced him on his journey. We see here and there, traces of Avery in how he handled shape, of Matisse and Hoffmann in how he handled color, and of Mondrian in how he eventually eliminated content. But the overall impression is one of many visions given many different expressions. Of many different strands, never entirely resolved. There seem to be many Diebenkorns. The Diebenkorn of the cityscape; the Diebenkorn of the threatening female figure, and the Diebenkorn of the empty ocean image. Each Diebenkorn is satisfying on the level he sets for himself. Each level has great strengths. But no level fully soars.

From the 40's through the 60's, Diebenkorn experiments with the vocabulary of the abstract movement. He uses the gamut of available measures. Abstract pattern against color fields, quirky line, drips, stains, textured brush strokes, and thick layers of paint applied by palette knife. He demonstrates great facility in combining these elements. The surfaces of the canvases sparkle.

Representational landscapes appear suddenly in the late 50's. Abstract elements dominate, as color and composition form major organizing structures. Two 1963 canvases, *Cityscape* and *Cityscape 1*, are particularly successful in the spatial interaction of shape.

Figures and interiors appear as well. In black and white drawings of the female, the process of drawing becomes part of the content. The figure is stretched into design shapes, much the way Matisse had done. But these are no Matisse *Odalisques*. Diebenkorn's women are almost as fearsome and aggressive as de Kooning's.

Interiors can be large and liquid. Color is limpid and is contrasted with black grillwork. These interiors have a beauty that again owes much to Matisse.

The work culminates in the *Ocean Park* series, the series for which the artist is best known. Here an underlying grid organizes the composition. Color is quiet. It is usually in pale cool hues, with lots of blues. There are echoes of Mondrian, Matisse and Hoffman. At times the canvases have a kaleidoscopic, almost stained glass quality. There is a spatial balance and something dreamlike about them. The work is hushed and quiet, even serene. There is a deliberate emptiness. But oddly, with so many of these canvases present, the emptiness starts to acquire a feeling of vacancy. There is a strange sensation, not of fulfillment, but of non-fulfillment. Of a surface with very little depths. Of no there there.

And odder still, the impression of the exhibit seems to be one of irresolution. Of differing visions that never quite cohere. Of different strands that, finally, never seem to have been fully integrated.

Gentle Indignation   **October 1997**

PISSARRO AT THE JEWISH MUSEUM

October, 1997

The Highly Opinionated Newsletter

Volume Two, Number 13

Camille Pissarro in the Caribbean at The Jewish Museum—This small show of drawings, many of which may or may not be by Pissarro, is surely a great oddity. And also an enigma. There is very little here of interest. And even less which can be attributed with certainty to the young Pissarro. There isn't that much difference either in technique or vision between the sketches of the young Pissarro and his teacher, Fritz Melbye. In drawing after drawing, we find little that is distinguished. Much less distinguishable between the two. This can be a dispiriting experience.

Wall placards imply that a general impressionistic slackness characterizes Pissarro's sketches. Try as I might, I could hardly find this a virtue.

The same placards imply that a greater precision and detail characterize work by Melbye. Unfortunately, I didn't find this much of a virtue, either.

What might possibly be the intention of the curators in presenting such a curious exhibit is anybody's guess. Other than to show their own ignorance, to display work of indifferent quality, and to demonstrate how difficult it is to attribute mediocre work amid confusing circumstances.

These hardly seem to me very good reasons to produce an exhibit. On the contrary, they seem to me very good reasons not to.

Gentle Indignation   October 1997

MONET AT THE BROOKLYN MUSEUM

November, 1997

The Highly Opinionated Newsletter

Volume Two, Number 14

Monet in the Mediterranean at the Brooklyn Museum—Has greed gone so far that a museum is not embarrassed to assemble a group of second-rate paintings? For the primary purpose of luring lots of visitors? Most of whom will look at the work and will not even know better?

That, I am afraid, is what has happened at the Brooklyn Museum's exhibition of paintings by Monet. The visitor goes from painting to painting in a vain search for something—anything—that rises above the level of the mediocre. But the mediocre is the norm for this show. There isn't one canvas to demonstrate anything like the magic of which Monet is capable.

Instead, we are presented with piece after piece of clumsy work. Work that lacks everything we have come to expect from great painting. There is a total absence of compositional strength. Shapes are either awkward or flimsy. Color, when not dull and tired, is painfully forced. Brushwork flails in ways that weaken work that is already weak. The worst faults of Monet are brought together here. In case we might otherwise have overlooked them.

Much of the work from 1884 on the Italian Riviera is loose and unstructured. In *Farm at Bordighera*, flabby brushstrokes frame fields of cloying green. In *Gardens of Bordighera*, large brownish clumps of foliage appear to writhe. Palm trees with ungainly forms clutter many canvases.

In only two canvases of olive trees do the tree trunks serve to anchor slack imagery.

The work on the French Riviera 1884–8 is, on the whole, as poor. In *Corniche of Monaco*, a wide red swath of road refuses to lie flat. Only in *Cap Martin* is there a reminder of Monet's ability to render light.

There is little that can be said about any of the works done in Venice, 1908. Other than that they are astonishingly underdeveloped. Even amateurish.

Monet can be one of the most remarkable of the Impressionist artists. Yet here he is represented by works which consistently lack sinew. Works so flaccid they fall apart.

Throughout his career, Monet made remarkable paintings. Paintings of often breathtaking beauty. Sadly enough, not one of them is here.

Gentle Indignation   **November 1997**

RAUSCHENBERG AT THE GUGGENHEIM

November, 1997

The Highly Opinionated Newsletter

Volume Two, Number 15

Rauschenberg at the Guggenheim—There is nothing the least self-effacing about any of Rauschenberg's art. Everything happens on a grandiose scale. Or bigger. Everything says notice me. And people do. People are pouring in to do just that. It's exactly the art they want. And exactly the art they deserve. It's art as extravaganza.

It's encyclopedic in scope. Rauschenberg deals in visual overload. Too much of a good thing or too much of a bad thing. It doesn't matter. The important thing is that there be too much. Material is so unexpected that we soon expect anything. Like a kind of successor to pop art and op art, this is *prop* art. There are ladders and crates, doors and mirrors. Lights, glass and metal. Fabric and sneakers. Pails, chains and tire treads. There are also objects straight from the mortuary. Like dead birds and a goat. About the only thing that's lacking is the proverbial kitchen sink. But Rauschenberg wouldn't deign to use anything so hackneyed. He likes to surprise. And he does. Unfortunately, so many surprises become tedious.

Rauschenberg combines his unusual materials in idiosyncratic ways. He frequently contrasts them with transfers appropriated from traditional art. The traditional art adds a much needed touch of class. And of beauty. Yes. Occasionally, amid the hurly burly, a touch of beauty emerges. It can emerge through color or through texture. Sometimes through shape and image.

The work in the 50's begins on a somewhat small and experimental scale. There is a rawness and a deliberate ugliness. But soon the work gets more ambitious. And larger. Then, despite an attempt to do otherwise, it becomes suave. Every layout is unerringly designed. Facility turns decidedly facile.

There is an emphasis on puns and palindromes. As in *Pneumonia Lisa* (1982) and *Able Was I Ere I Saw Elba* (1985). The art becomes self-referential. Cleverness is its own subject. The artist may not tire of such wit and ingenuity. But *we* do.

Ironically, then, the cumulative effect of this huge show is mind-numbing. Mental gymnastics start to wear thin. Visual counterparts do not sustain interest. An art of such banality shows the banality of such art. It all gets to seem too full of sound and fury. And to signify nothing much.

Gentle Indignation   **November 1997**

FILIPPINO LIPPI AT THE METROPOLITAN MUSEUM

November, 1997

The Highly Opinionated Newsletter

Volume Two, Number 16

Filippino Lippi at MMA—The drawings of Filippino Lippi, 1457–1504, reflect a kinder gentler time. Aesthetic standards were still high and artists strove to meet them. Filippino was fortunate enough to be apprenticed to artists such as Botticelli for the purpose of learning how to draw the human figure with beauty and dignity. Judging from this exhibit, he learned well.

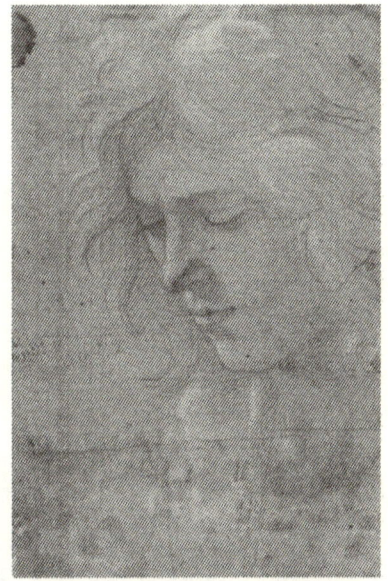

Filippino Lippi's work may be seen as having three phases. The early phase displays the influence of Botticelli. Then, as Filippino's work develops, that influence wanes. Yet no vision of corresponding strength emerges. There is a sense instead of an artist adrift. Decorative elements clutter the work. Later, as the impact of Leonardo is felt, the work acquires new strength. The

Filippino Lippi, Head of a Young Man Turned to the Left and Looking Down, ca. 1480-83 [metalpoint, heightened with white gouach, on red-tinted paper; 7 3/8" x 4 13/16"]

artist readjusts the way he sees and the way he represents what he sees. Line takes on stronger, more gestural qualities. Gone is the delicacy of contour associated with early work. But gone along with that is the very quality we have come most to admire.

Among early work, both *Head of a Young Woman* and *Head of Young Man Turned to the Left and Looking Down* have a special aura. The heads appear luminous, as ineffable and exquisite as gossamer. These works acknowledge the tender conjunction of youth and beauty. In *Standing Male Nude Facing Left and Leaning on a Staff*, the androgyny of that conjunction is depicted.

Pairs of figures interact graciously. Stance and gesture display amplitude and grace. Touches of thought and emotion imbue finely modeled features. The *Kneeling St. Mary Magdelen and Standing Christ* portrays both supplication and support, as frailty beseeches strength for protection.

But problems appear as the work continues. The once remarkable sense of weightlessness acts to dilute figures. The highlighting of folds and of musculature seems overwrought and florid. Parts distract from and conflict with the whole. Decorative elements abound. In *Four Seated Male Nudes*, figures dissolve into vague pools of ghostly light. In larger sketches, groups lack focus.

Then later in the 1490's, the work of Leonardo reinspires Filippino. His own work undergoes a change. Contours are less precise and more general. A new energy empowers the weighted and unified figures.

And so as we view these drawings, we note how even toward the end of a distinguished career, Filippino Lippi is still seeking. Still apprenticing himself. Still learning from masters. And we are touched.

*   *   *

A few drawings by Raphael conclude the show. Each one is unerring in its simplicity and poignancy. Their mere presence serves to illuminate at once Filippino's shortcomings.

Gentle Indignation   **November 1997**

Picasso at the Boston Museum of Fine Arts

November, 1997

The Highly Opinionated Newsletter

Volume Two, Number 17

Picasso: The Early Years at the Boston Museum of Fine Arts—Anytime one approaches an exhibition on Picasso, one must be prepared to be surprised. Which Picasso will be on view? There are so many and they are so varied that it is hard to know. This exhibition is arranged in seven parts. Each part presents a different Picasso.

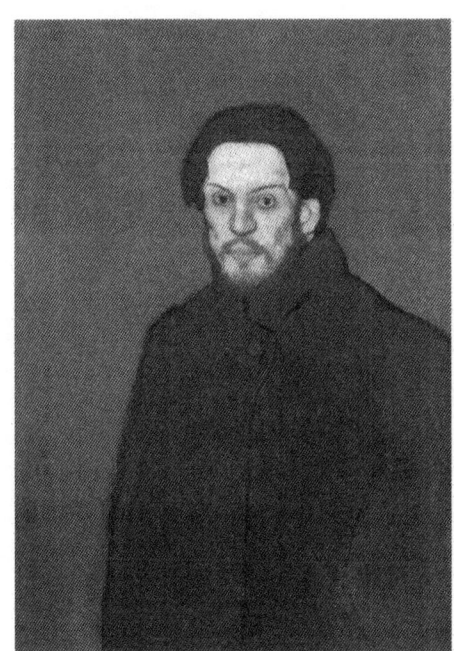

Pablo Picasso, Self-Portrait, 1901
[oil on canvas; 31 7/8" x 23 5/8"]

The first gallery displays the work of Picasso the child. The 1893 *Study of a Torso After a Plaster Cast*, done at the age of twelve, shows that Picasso was born knowing everything there is to know about technique. Line, modeling, weight, composition, proportion and perspective. It all comes easily. In figure representation. And in landscape, although it is far weaker. An 1896 youthful *Self-Portrait* gazes out at us quizzically.

In the following two sections: "Avant-Garde Barcelona" and "Experimenting 1901", Picasso seems lost. A surprising vapidity marks many of the drawings and paintings, which show little of the familiar Picasso energy. A 1901 painting, *Child Holding a Dove*, captures the innocence and sweetness of an imagined childhood through arresting color and imagery. In a *Self-Portrait* (1901), the unnatural white of the artist's head contrasts starkly against a black coat and blue background. The expression now is one of confrontation, even defiance.

Works from the Blue Period, when seen together, appear somewhat obvious and melodramatic. During the Rose Period, a new poetry softens the figures. Picasso's mistress Madeleine serves as muse and her visage combines tenderness with strength. Figures are stretched and angled. Long, thin fingers appear as eloquent as features do. In the 1904 *Frugal Repast*, the figures form a unit both of comfort and of isolation. In *Woman Ironing*, the whitened torso becomes a geometric medley of angles and lines.

The circus world seems to me to be the artist's finest and most original contribution. The world is a hermetic and self-contained one. The figures in it have assigned roles. They reenact various stages of life from childhood, adolescence and adulthood. Occasions range from birth through death. These figures seem both alien and familiar. For behind the costumes and performance, it is ourselves that we are viewing. We are both the observer and the observed.

From 1905 onward, Picasso again changes idiom. In the "Mediterranean Classicism" Period, canvases take on the color of earth. Outlined figures of rounded women are set like terra-cotta sculptures. They, too, are of the earth. They have the timelessness and iconic quality of the eternal female: preening and erotic, nurturing and seducing.

In "Toward A New Figure Painting", simplification of color and shape continues. In the well-known *Portrait of Gertrude Stein* (1906), that writer's visage is reduced to and rendered as an inscrutable mask. In his 1906 *Self-Portrait With Palette*, Picasso likewise erases himself, leaving before us a blank visage and a vacant stare. It is as if he, too, is bewildered by himself. By his many personalities and modes of expression. As if he, too, must take time out to find out, if he can, what he may never know any more than we do. Just who is he anyway?

And this is ultimately both the great fascination and the singular problem with Picasso. For we can never fully separate Picasso the man from Picasso the artist. He never lets us. Both are always present everywhere in his work. The two are inseparable.

And the question is never fully resolved. Not in his life. Nor in his art. Just who is Picasso anyway? Aside from the fact that he was an artist of genius possessed with a formidable technique, we can never know. There are too many incompatible answers. And there is no one transcendent vision.

Gentle Indignation   **November 1997**

BONNARD AND NADELMAN AT SALANDER O'REILLY

December, 1997

The Highly Opinionated Newsletter

Volume Two, Number 18

Bonnard and Nadelman at Salander-O'Reilly—This selection of Bonnard's work is small and uneven. The best canvases glow with blocks of solid color. In *Bord de Mer* (1923), the intensity of a tangerine island is set against a blue-green background. In *Paysage du Midi* (1910), the yellows of the background somehow open up against the foreground browns. In other work, color arrangement sparkles unexpectedly; and black lines form sinuous trees.

But many canvases are simply uninteresting. *Le Pin Solitaire* (1923) lacks focal point. Here, as elsewhere, color and composition are weak. And mostly, there is a staleness, a feeling of having seen it all before.

Nadelman's sculpture is meticulously built up from soft and exaggerated geometric shapes. In the best pieces, there can be a quirky humor, as in the 1913 *Horse*. Its inflated shape is perched comically atop slim and elegant legs. Female sculptures are both massive and voluptuous. But highly detailed hair and hands strike a discordant note. Gestures are overly exact, even mannered. The effect can seem contrived or sentimental. A series of sculpted heads seem blurred. Eyes are closed and features erased. These heads seem more about facade than about personality. They are unsettling. A large 1935 *Standing Woman* combines overt sexuality with coyness. A 1925 *Seated Female Figure* is the epitome of prim.

But on the way out of the gallery, I passed a first or second century Roman *Aphrodite*. Her simply modeled torso came as a reproach and a relief.

Gentle Indignation   **December 1997**

JACKSON POLLACK AT THE METROPOLITAN MUSEUM

December, 1997

The Highly Opinionated Newsletter

Volume Two, Number 19

Jackson Pollock at MMA—These pages are taken from Pollock's student sketchbooks, 1937–1941. What facility there is is displayed primarily in copies of Michelangelo's figures from the Sistine Chapel, with their strong linear quality.

But there is nothing else of consequence. When Pollock is not borrowing from Michelangelo and is on his own, there is little that is inspired. Drawing turns heavy-handed and crude. Figures become structured into cubelike forms. Strange flamelike patterns in brownish tones appear as background. There seems to be both an inability and a disinterest in refining representational skill. Meaningless markings assemble themselves into depressing semblances of composition. It all seems to happen aimlessly, almost by default.

But the sketchbooks do accomplish one thing. They enable us to understand why Pollock decided to abandon traditional means of representation. For within their pages we can see how unable he was to make representation work meaningfully for him. And how consequently, even at the beginning, he was drawn to non-representation as an alternative means of expression.

Gentle Indignation   December 1997

PICASSO AT THE MUSEUM OF MODERN ART

December, 1997

The Highly Opinionated Newsletter

Volume Two, Number 20

Picasso the Engraver, Musee Picasso, at MMA—Another Picasso exhibit? Why not? There's plenty left to fill exhibits such as this and many more. For Picasso is a source of inexhaustible invention and energy. And contradiction. All of which appear in this show, which traces his development as an engraver. From the earliest example, the 1904 *Frugal Repast* through the work of the 1930's, we see Picasso as he wrestles with his great themes. Contradictory themes embracing the whole of the human condition. Themes on the role of

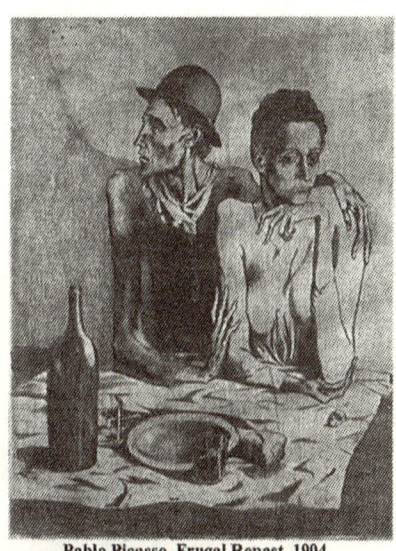

Pablo Picasso, Frugal Repast, 1904
[etching; 18¼" x 14 7/8"]

nature as both benign and destructive. On men and women as antagonists and lovers. And on the role of the artist as observer of disorder and creator of order. All portrayed with breathtaking facility. Sometimes with beauty. Sometimes with anger. Always with wit.

The 1904 *Frugal Repast* is an indelible image of stoic alienation, with angular heads and fingers emphasizing the plight. The woodblock *Nudes* of the 1920's are playful and linear. Mythological themes are important and are conveyed with authority and conviction. The 1929

Bull represents nature at its most inscrutably powerful. The 1933 *Serenade* series contains thirty-three variations on a single theme. That theme is art and the artist. It is also the tangible and the intangible, spirit and flesh. The series, like the music it represents, grows progressively more abstracted.

The work in the 1930's reflects a growing unease and dissatisfaction. There are twenty-eight variations on his mistress Marie Therese (1933). Each one of them is ugly. The 1933 *Marie Therese Dreaming* is a reverie about the complex relationship between artist and model. As well as about man's conflicting impulses to ravish and to protect. The extraordinary 1934 *Tauromachy*, with its interlocking figures forever contending, continues the dialogue between violence and innocence.

The 1935 *Minotauromachy* casts the human condition in terms of darks and lights, evil and innocence, victimizers and victims. The minotaur is the excessively masculine aspect: violence unleashed. The feminine aspect is childlike, wielding the glow of everything pure.

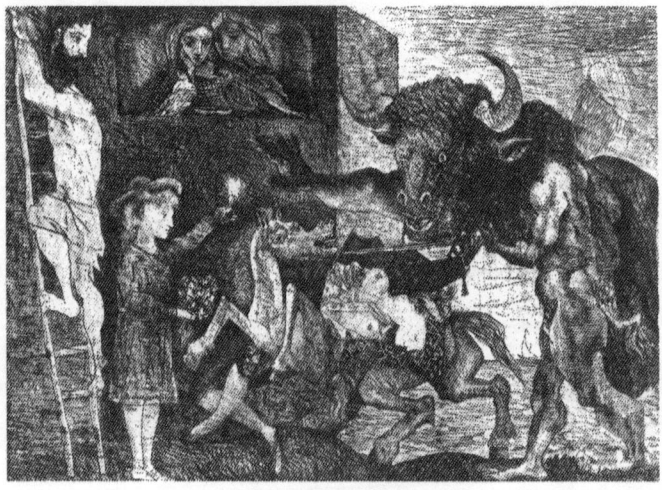

Pablo Picasso, Minotauromachia, 1935 [etching; 19¼" x 27 5/8"]

In ensuing work, woman becomes a complex symbol. Also a projection of inner conflict, of hopes and of fears. She is alternately tender as in the 1936 *Faun and Sleeping Woman*. And threatening, as in the 1937 *Weeping* Woman disfigured by psychic anguish. Woman becomes iconic in scope. She is simultaneously alluring and threatening; seductive and repulsive. The discord is real. And never symbolically resolved.

And that, in the end, is what is so disquieting about Picasso. The world he occupies is one of great disorder. He is unable to accept this. But all his genius cannot alter it. And so the reaction depicted is too often one of frustration, anger and fear.

Gentle Indignation   **December 1997**

AFTERWORD

IN CONCLUSION: The essential point to remember is that there *is* no conclusion. Art is an ongoing process to which each generation adds as it evaluates and reevaluates all that previous generations have bequeathed. Each generation decides anew what is of value and why. And then this, too, is open to question by future generations. In this way, we all take part in creating the sum total of what is worthy to be valued as art.

To be continued....

INDEX OF ARTISTS

0-595-21899-7

www.ingramcontent.com/pod-product-compliance
Lightning Source LLC
Chambersburg PA
CBHW030930180526
45163CB00002B/513